EXECUTIVE DIRECTOR
Suzanne Tise-Isoré
Style & Design Collection

EDITORIAL COORDINATION
Lara Lo Calzo

GRAPHIC DESIGN
Bernard Lagacé

COPY EDITING
Lindsay Porter

PROOFREADING
Clodagh Kinsella

PRODUCTION
Élodie Conjat

COLOR SEPARATION
Les Artisans du Regard, Paris

PRINTING
Verona Libri, Italy

Simultaneously published in French
as *Tino Zervudachi, Autour du monde.*

Flammarion S.A.
82, rue Saint-Lazare
75009 Paris
editions.flammarion.com
@styleanddesignflammarion

22 23 24 3 2 1
ISBN: 978-2-08-026212-7
Legal Deposit: 10/2022

CONTENTS

FRONT COVER
Tino's New York apartment where McCollin Bryan's circular pendulum mirror backdrop reflects the hallway, a Robsjohn-Gibbings chair, and a pair of chairs by André Sornay. The nineteenth-century Thai gilt-bronze figure of Shakyamuni Buddha and the green mohair flat-weave carpet is custom from Sacco Carpet New York.

PAGE 2
From left, in the Tino Zervudachi Paris office, a dark patinated nineteenth-century plaster cast of Egyptian pharaoh Ramses II and a 1940s Italian table, along with an art piece of the Palais-Royal, by Langlands & Bell, and a bronze sculpture of a stag by François Pompon, create the hallway's congenial atmosphere.

PAGE 3
A curved staircase, restored and enlarged by Tino and Jim de Missolf, is a central feature of his office, a former artist's studio built in the early twentieth century.

PAGE 4
Under the painted architectural beams of his office, Tino sits on an eighteenth-century English dining chair at his 1940s macassar ebony table, flanked by a pair of Thebes stools and a leg-shaped Robert Couturier bronze standing lamp with a foot-shaped base.

PAGE 5
The exterior of Tino Zervudachi's office, which is set in the heart of the rue de Grenelle in the seventh arrondissement in Paris.

FACING PAGE
A perspective drawing of a project by Ohm Wittawat Chulsukon, a partner in Tino's Paris office.

FOREWORD

DERRY MOORE

It is a particular pleasure to write about Tino Zervudachi, as I played a very small part in the start of his career. When he was seventeen, his mother told me that he was applying to art school and was looking for a job until term started. Knowing of his interest in photography, I suggested that he assist me as I was going to photograph an apartment that my friend, the famous interior designer David Mlinaric, had just finished. Tino, although interested in photography, had never worked as a photographic assistant before, but he immediately understood what was needed and at the end of the day, David was so impressed that he asked if I could find someone to work for him who was as efficient as Tino. The answer was obvious; Tino joined David's firm, later became a partner, and then, when David decided to retire, eventually bought the firm, which became known as Mlinaric, Henry and Zervudachi, or simply MHZ. However, it's one thing to be given a timely introduction—to take advantage of such a moment is much, much harder and Tino most definitely did just that.

When I consider the qualities that have made him so successful, there are certain features that stand out: he has an outstanding gift for making interior spaces work, which in the final analysis is far more important than the decoration of a place, since if the overall design is poor the decoration can only mask the shortcomings, not remedy them. He is also extremely accomplished in the practical side of interior design, as well as contemporary technology, both elements that are never to be underestimated. Work on his own house up a steep hill in Greece is a good example of this. The project required not only overcoming the logistics of building up a steep hillside, involving literally hundreds of journeys up and down, using mules as the only means of transporting the building materials, but also all the normal logistical problems, which are magnified many times on a Greek island. Added to this, he had to negotiate the labyrinthine intricacies and procrastinations of the Greek Archaeological Service, a process which makes many people give up in despair. Tino, luckily, does not lack perseverance.

Another of his qualities is his outstanding ability both to understand his clients' needs and to empathize with them. His clients enjoy his company, although I must emphasize that his charm in no way diminishes his professional capabilities. He also manages, within the range of his designs, to encompass many different styles, according to the period of house. He incorporates his knowledge of period and decorative style into the atmosphere of a room, with the result that the room looks as if it had evolved naturally.

Tino works internationally and his skill in adapting and creating designs that reflect the environment—in the United States, for example, in France, or on a Greek island—is considerable. He is equally at home on water and has designed the interiors of several yachts. None of this would be possible without that most enviable of qualities—energy—which enables him to travel constantly, often taking several flights a week, having meetings, and making site visits, as well as creating designs and overseeing them—and, as he has many projects on the go at the same time, retaining all of them in his head.

Two more characteristics of Tino are his optimism and enthusiasm. And in addition to these many and varied accomplishments, Tino Zervudachi is someone whose company is always a pleasure.

INTRODUCTION

NATASHA A. FRASER

Paris—arriving at Tino Zervudachi's HQ, its nautical elegance catches the eye. Innovative, the interior designer has made a feature of the hallway's steep, narrow staircase. Lit up by shell-inspired sconces, the polished steps invite, as do the curve of the industrial handrail and other Tino touches, such as the smart burgundy stripe on the smoothly painted walls and the stair risers painted different shades of blue. Instead of feeling pokey and strange, the hallway has become shipshape and glamorous. It illustrates the flare and the ease associated with the fifty-nine-year-old, who freely admits, "I do sort of believe in reinventing the wheel for each project."

Tino's relentless determination and exacting taste have forged his forty-year career, and he counts an enviable client list of art collectors, billionaire tycoons, and bohemian aristocrats. All the while, Tino has quietly etched an international reputation that spans projects from Paris, London, and New York to Athens, Connecticut, Delhi, Gstaad, Hydra, Ibiza, Los Angeles, Lyford Cay, Montenegro, Mustique, Rio, Toronto, Tokyo, and more. This constant activity explains the three Tino Zervudachi & Associés (TZA) offices flourishing in Paris, London, and New York, a dream team of business partners consisting of Antoine de Haut de Sigy, Marie-Astrid Piron, and Ohm Wittawat Chulsukon in Paris; Lucy Singh in New York; and Jason Roberts and Laurence Macadam in London. "Experience makes you a team player," Tino says. "You recognize your strengths and weaknesses and realize what fun it is to work together and learn to delegate."

Although Tino Zervudachi was one of the first interior designers to be included in the same year in the top 100 lists of American *Architectural Digest*, French *Architectural Digest*, and British *House & Garden*, he is not of the diva mold. Instead of arriving at design meetings with teams of staff, Tino is much more understated, rarely traveling with more than one assistant, if any. This low-key demeanor can disarm. "The first time we met, I remember thinking, 'Can he really be that nice?' and I was initially a bit suspicious," says the financier Nat Rothschild, who has commissioned double-digits projects, including a couple of yachts. Peter Simon, meanwhile, is impressed by Tino Zervudachi's work ethic. "Our second day in Mustique, Tino sat there, started sketching, and had ideas that I never would have thought of," says the collector and billionaire retailer. Nate McBride, on the other hand, appreciates Tino Zervudachi's micro and macro range. "Tino can pull back and have a bird's-eye view of the project and then fly into the detail," says the New York-based architect. "He really understands how people move and feel."

Tino's gentle way with clients rarely fails. He sounds out, encourages, and guides them to adventure. A bond will be made. Talk to Tino's coterie of clients and they remain enchanted. "It's his genuine simplicity and lovely manners," says Anne Gibson. There is the openness. "Since Tino is receptive and curious, I think you can say or propose anything to him," says Tatiana Casiraghi. Tino Zervudachi

adapts to his clients. "He doesn't reproduce Tino everywhere," says Laure Sudreau. "He listens and doesn't impose his taste." Many appreciate the quick instinct. "He gets your personality and respects who you are," says Arielle de Rothschild, an investment banker. There is also the harmony that drives each project. "Tino manages the process so beautifully," says George Duffield. "He also fixes problems and makes the house work." Most clients return again and again. "When I did try and use someone else, I immediately came back to Tino with my tail between my legs," reveals Nat Rothschild.

By his own estimation, Tino Zervudachi is "a different Tino for every project." His extensive experience has taught him so much, he approaches new projects with a fresh eye. Yet it is hard to disagree with Louis-Charles de Remusat, his partner of twenty-five years, that "Tino is a serious person who doesn't take himself seriously" and that "he's motored by optimism, curiosity, and passion." This becomes evident when walking around Tino's elegant Paris HQ in the seventh arrondissement: a purpose-built, early twentieth-century former artist's studio building. Humming with activity, the company's every aspect evokes his universe, ranging from the hushed tones, to the young architects poring over plans, the measured lineup of marble and tile samples, the well-stacked reference library, the wall of box files packed with textiles, and all the framed magazine covers confined to the kitchen.

Tino's office on the top floor is reached by a graceful, curving metal staircase. Light-filled with lofty ceilings and painted, structural timber beams, it has a rooftop view of an eighteenth-century building across an unexpected garden. Contemporary, the room marries well with Tino's choice of objects, which include a nineteenth-century Suzani wall hanging, a cloisonné chest by André Dubreuil, a plaster lamp by Alberto Giacometti, and a pencil drawing by Geoffrey Bennison, whose whimsy contrasts with the large glass and iron conference table, and 1950s PEL leather chairs, acquired thirty-six years ago for his first apartment. The arrangement reminds one of Tino's insistence on uniqueness. "I find repetition difficult to justify, because clients are paying for my ideas," he says.

In Benjamin Steinitz's opinion, the lack of Zervudachi template originates from a burning need for creative stimulation. "When you look at his projects that span Tokyo, New York, or Gstaad, for instance, they all have their own identity and their own chic," he says. Tatiana Casiraghi, however, puts it down to his enthusiasm and an ability to both develop and enhance a client's vision. "Tino was very excited by my choice of prints, colors, and ideas behind creating a Russian dacha vibe," she says. "My project was different to his others. Tino had his set of ideas but was open to mine. He really appreciated my mood boards and helped me develop the concept." Constantin Contacuzène, who worked in Zervudachi's Paris and London offices for six years, sees in this ever-evolving attitude an aim to create soulful interiors and avoid mediocrity. "Tino does not care about fashion or

FACING PAGE, CLOCKWISE, FROM TOP LEFT A portrait of Tino, taken in London by Ambroise Tézenas; his office's entrance hall, lit by a Tino Zervudachi-designed plaster light fixture and Manuela Zervudachi-sculpted shell sconces; the meeting area in Tino's studio with large glass table and modernist 1950s PEL leather chairs.

following trends," says the Swiss-based decorator. "He creates spaces that defend a point of view, where there is vision and in which a conversation exists between all the elements."

Meanwhile, a sensitivity to history is a key part of Tino's modus operandi. A spontaneous architect, he follows the balance of rooms, but subtly modernizes. Laure Sudreau applauds the approach. "He does a fantastic job of rearranging and making it look like it has been like that forever," says the French lawyer-turned-film producer and financier. Tino's gift for revitalizing has transformed grand European houses; he has brought a beloved family château into the twenty-first century, but he has also collaborated in building a cut-stone Connecticut-style farmhouse from scratch, to look as if it has existed for one hundred years. Andrew Oyen, an architect colleague of fifteen years, puts it down to a combination of high-mindedness and a sense of story. "Tino has a foot in the past and a foot in the present," says the New York-based architect, associated with Oscar Shamamian of the architectural firm Ferguson & Shamamian.

Tino's enthusiasm for color and attention to detail lend warmth to his interiors. "New York designers are known for a certain palette, like mouse gray," says Kathy Jones from La Regence upholstery atelier. "Never with Tino. Bright blue, plum, yellow..." There is also the tactile dimension of Tino's rooms, achieved by ultra-refined choice of textiles. "Since he uses old mill fabrics, it makes them refreshing and wild," Jones says. The designer's fondness for a tightly loomed jacquard, taking years to create, as well as using fabric on walls, are equally noteworthy. "You can't get that effect with plaster and/or paint," Jones states.

Zervudachi's signature use of textiles for chairs, cushions as well as his use of carpets, adds further texture to his carefully crafted, architecturally thoughtful interiors. Often upholstered with exquisite details, Tino's chairs are little works of art, his careful arrangement of cushions enhance comfort, while his way with carpets has has launched much-imitated trends. Usually self-designed, then woven by manufacturers such as Marcel Zelmanovitch at Paris's Galerie Diurne, they offer depth and make the room approachable.

Chairs, cushions, and carpets marry Tino's nuanced hues and sense of luxury. They also informalize a serious collection. "He succeeds in regrouping really important art," says Steinitz. "At the same time, it is not done in a light way." In Thaddaeus Ropac's opinion, this ease and confidence stem from Tino Zervudachi being a collector—from "The way Tino sees exhibitions, carefully looks, and gets involved," the art gallerist says. "It's obvious that he's been embracing art for a long time."

This knowledge contributes to Tino's flexibility. "There are some designers, you have to share their vision and it's difficult if you don't," says Ropac. "But Tino was very happy to share ideas, in the most wonderful way." Optimistic, Tino Zervudachi also envisions potential. "I was rather embarrassed by my new house in Mustique," says Peter Simon. "It seemed really too basic in comparison to his other projects. And Tino said, 'Look Peter, we're going to make it special because it has the most spectacular location.'" It's architectural shortfalls will be managed by the new design to create an exceptionally well located, elegant beach house by the careful rearrangement of indoor and outdoor spaces and the selection of more appropriate new finishes.

Tino Zervudachi can also financially downsize. When working on the Porto Montenegro project—which meant transforming an old naval repair facility into a luxurious village of three hundred apartments, including the five-star Regent hotel, separate penthouses, and five hundred berths—Tino was hailed for turning an exceedingly tight budget into something that resembled an unlimited one. "I was running Montenegro as a commercial beast," says Oliver Corlette, the then financial manager. "And Tino's attitude was always, 'How can we get twice the effect, for half the amount?'"

Then there's the legendary TZ stamina. "He'll come to dinner, and you'll realize that Tino has just jumped out of the plane and has been traveling for the past three weeks," says Benjamin Steinitz. His only criticism concerns the designer's almost vault-like discretion. "I try to torture and tease information out of him, but Tino still won't tell me," he says. James Reginato readily agrees. "Something of a sphinx, he guards his clients well," the author says.

FAR LEFT
In Paris's seventh arrondissement, in the living room, a Manuela Zervudachi *Space Cloud* sculpture made out of terra-cotta with Chinese lacquer and pigment patina as well as a Galerie Diurne rug specially designed for the space in a set of three by Tino Zervudachi.

LEFT
In a castle hallway Tino Zervudachi designed a vaulted ceiling, and rough plaster walls with contrast-painted borders to create an atmosphere of times past. Cast-iron lanterns and built-in wall sconces light the space.

TOP RIGHT
The Indian-inspired lacquered bar in the private dining room at Mark's Club, with ebonized chairs, and the walls upholstered and Dior-pleated in red silk, designed by Tino in 2016 and described as "the haven of exclusivity."

FACING PAGE
BOTTOM LEFT
A perspective drawing for a contemporary house in Athens.

BOTTOM RIGHT
Private house in Rio filled exclusively with Brazilian-designed and -made furniture, like the Guilherme Torres tables and Sergio Rodrigues chairs.

The secrecy can surprise. "I had no idea that Tino had a twin until I found Manuela Zervudachi's work on the internet—a tremendous discovery—and asked if she was a relation," recalls Arielle de Rothschild. "He's far from pushy." Although the Zervudachi siblings are very close, it is Tino's office that informs her of his awards, contracts, and glowing magazine articles. "Usually, Tino hasn't told me," she says.

The Zervudachi twins were educated at the French Lycée in London's South Kensington and brought up by their Irish mother and Greek father in a large house in Holland Park with their two elder brothers. In tribute to their family's background, vacations were spent in Egypt with their paternal grandparents. The siblings became privy to the Zervudachi's once-fabled Alexandria existence in their grandmother's 1930s apartment, which was filled with furniture that had decorated a previous apartment designed by Maison Jansen, the celebrated Paris-based interior decorator active in the 1940s. Tino and Manuela would chase after a pet chameleon on the veranda, in between the cane furniture. Afternoons were spent at the family's cabana, situated on Montazah Palace's golden, sandy beach. Their grandfather had refined taste, with an exquisite sense of style, having immaculate leather cases made for all his everyday objects. "That attention to detail was inspiring," Tino says.

Tino discovered exceptional interiors when he was twelve. He leafed through piles of American design magazines while staying with family friends in their elegant villa by the sea in Greece. Three years later, the antique dealer Adrian Ward-Jackson commissioned Tino to photograph his eighteenth- and nineteenth-century paintings and objets d'art for his catalogs. Wearing ripped jeans and Converse trainers, the fifteen-year-old Tino, who had taken up photography with a passion, would turn up at Ward-Jackson's grand Mayfair apartment. "It was a world of efficient, immaculately dressed secretaries, the phone ringing, and elegant ladies coming in to buy their treasures, that inspired and taught me about exceptional high quality art," he says.

These rarefied circumstances prepared Tino for his next mentor—David Mlinaric, the legendary interior designer.

As Derry Moore's foreword reveals, they were introduced at a magazine shoot at the home of the photographer Patrick Lichfield. "In those days, you didn't have Photoshop," says Mlinaric. "You had to be absolutely precise when composing a photograph and I remember looking at this young assistant (the eighteen-year-old Tino) and being impressed by his level of observation." Tino was swiftly hired. "Even then, he had this way with people. Talking in the same way to the client as he did to the builder," recalls Mlinaric. "Full of energy, it was quite clear from the beginning that he could jump from one job to another and that he was incredibly particular. What people would call a fusspot. Now, I'm a fusspot, but it was then unusual in England."

Tino's first assignment was helping David Mlinaric on Curzon House, John Aspinall's extremely grand private gambling club in London. It was followed by the British Embassy in Paris, then the Nostell Priory in North Yorkshire. At his side, Tino learnt about Mlinaric's sense of rigor. "How to approach a building, what to look out for, what to be concerned about, what to care about," Tino says. "It was simply the very best training." Keen to further educate his apprentice, Mlinaric asked an architect friend to give drawing classes to Tino. "But after a bit, Richard said, 'Tino doesn't need them. He's already over and above that.'"

In 1984 and at the age of twenty-one, Tino acquired his first client. She was an elegant, London-based Greek who had recently acquired a small but grand house in Kensington, which had a front and back garden that would be designed by François Goffinet. "It was a daunting first project because there was no architect," Tino says. His travels even took him to Paris, where he sourced fabrics from the Madeleine Castaing shop. After seeing the house, Mlinaric was so astounded—his words being, "I just cannot believe what Tino has done"—that he called Piers von Westenholz, his best friend and antiques dealer, to discuss it.

This assignment was quickly followed by a grand folly in Norfolk for Ivor Braka, the revered art dealer and collector. "It became an exhilarating collaboration," enthuses Tino. "Since it was a fractured house, our goal was to smooth the tension between grandeur and simplicity," Tino recalls. Once again,

Tino managed the whole project without an architect. Afterward, Braka commissioned Tino to design his house in London, his vacation home in Saint-Tropez, and then a further property there, fusing two village houses together. "Since Ivor was after an exotic atmosphere, we sourced architectural elements and furniture from Marrakech," says Tino. An elaborate process, it led to bringing in Moroccan tilers in order to craft the traditional and highly intricate Zellige tiling. "Some pieces were so small that they had to be fixed in place using tweezers," he says.

During that period, Tino befriended distinguished members of decoration's old guard, like Geoffrey Bennison, Madeleine Castaing, David Hicks, and landscape gardener Alvilde Lees-Milne. "Now they've all gone," he says. "Even Colefax and Fowler in Brook Street has disappeared." He feels lucky to have known it all. "They were part of my life, my professional upbringing, and my inspiration," he continues.

After assisting Mlinaric on Mick Jagger's eighteenth-century château in the Val de Loire, Tino worked on the rock star's homes in London and Paris. When reimagining the bathroom, he used the glass and mirrored elements of a 1926 Lalique bathroom that were purchased by Jagger in the 1970s, and which for years had been stored in a barn.

After eight years of working in London on projects in the UK, the USA, and France, Tino was keen to open an office in Paris. Through a family friend, a perfect and stylish haven was found in the Palais-Royal. "When I first showed the office to David to get his approval, he completely understood how marvelous it was. 'It is world class,' he said, and was excited about the new adventure." Tino compares the 1990 move to "turning on a light in a dark room." He felt a kinship with the Parisian passion for detail and quality, refusal to put up with second-best, and impossibly high standards. Within no time, Tino gathered his band of artists and artisans, which still includes the sculptor Philippe Anthonioz, the painter Laurent Chwast, Marcel Zelmanovitch at Galerie Diurne, and also Tino's twin sister. "Within two seconds, he'll do a drawing, giving the measurements without looking at anything," says Manuela Zervudachi. "He just has it all inside his head."

TOP LEFT
18-foot (5.5 meter)—high windows—curtained in Claremont Ottoman stripe with toggle fringes, held within eyebrow-shaped Chippendale-inspired gilded timber pelmets—dominate the drawing room at Gunton Tower, Norfolk, England.

TOP RIGHT
To create the Moroccan-inspired bathroom in a private London home, Tino used Zellige tiles and designed a Moorish dressing room, with arched openings and painted canvas blinds.

CLOCKWISE, FROM TOP LEFT
In a double-height artist's studio in London's Chelsea, bespoke woven silk commissioned from Prelle forms the curtains with elaborate tie backs. The two 1950s glass chandeliers are from Barovier & Toso. The Tino Zervudachi-designed sweeping staircase in the White Cube jewelry shop in Vaduz, Liechtenstein, with a specially commissioned chandelier by Finnish artist Ilkka Suppanen.

The indoor pool at the Regent hotel in Montenegro: bespoke furniture and lighting complement the vaulted ceilings and columned archways. In a château in the Val de Loire, a newly designed staircase in he extended tower.

CLOCKWISE, FROM TOP LEFT
A Tino Zervudachi-designed plaster light fixture formed as a textured glass-bottomed bucket. A Parisian bathroom designed to incorporate original 1930s art deco carved- glass elements, with frosted mirror walls and etched-mirror floor tiles. Panton chairs and a Molteni table in a Chelsea kitchen, with a family porcelain collection, displayed by Bouke de Vries.

FACING PAGE
The spa pool with special fiber-optic "high lux" lighting projector by Swarovski at the prize-winning hotel Aurelio, Lech, Austria.

Over the past three decades, Tino's projects have progressed and exploded onto another level, essentially creating an interior design empire that boasts six business partners. When interviewing the latter, they refer to Tino's curiosity, work ethic, and respect. "He won't do Versailles in China," says Ohm Wittawat Chulsukon, from the Paris office. The TZA atmosphere remains close-knit. "We're more of a professional family than anything else," says Marie-Astrid Piron, in Paris. "Every partner—whatever the city—has their place." Everyone agrees that the unity comes from Tino. "Very personable, he spins the wheel as well as having the inside track to London, Paris, and New York," says Jason Roberts from the London office. "In our business, it's unusual to have a tactician who knows the technical side and is a really good team player." Still, Zervudachi is very much the star. "It's best that you let him be brilliant," continues Roberts. "That said, Tino is unusual for being charismatic and also sensitive; he's not a steamroller." Ohm Wittawat Chulsukon admires Tino's light way of gauging a client and being directive. "There's a depth that comes from his breath of knowledge as well as the symmetry and order of his work." Meanwhile, Tino is admired for his bravery and openness to new ideas. "If ever there's an opportunity to do something different, he'll jump on it," notes Laurence Macadam in the London office. "Tino is eternally curious and that's contagious." Being a TZA business partner defines the word "demanding." "Tino pushes to the nth degree," says Lucy Singh, in the New York office. "But we are all desperate to do our best for him. And the caliber of work is so thrilling, as is the level of artisanry." Singh is also stimulated by the lack of TZ signature style—"Tino just doesn't have one," she says—and his extraordinary memory: "He'll say, 'Remember that rug that we moved from that room?' And it will be years back." Though the hours are long and weekend emails are the norm, Singh stresses the joy and laughter. Antoine de Sigy, who runs the Paris office, highlights the trust and care. "Tino delegates and he's very good at letting you do your work," he says. Meanwhile, "his vast culture and immense energy" constantly surprise. "Tino never wants to do the same thing twice," says de Sigy. Last-minute changes can exasperate, but are saved by Zervudachi's uniqueness. "He brings a magic to the project that reflects the client," says Piron. "As I was telling an artisan, 'Tino does change his mind but it helps the situation and the design to

evolve.'" All the partners agree that their work is both elevated and exciting. "We don't think of ourselves as a brand, but we spend a lot of energy together, sounding each other out and problem solving," says Jason Roberts. "It matters to Tino that we get on. He's a bit of a hippy, at heart."

In 2010, complicated projects included creating a James Bond-like mansion with the Japanese architect Kengo Kuma. But that sounds straightforward in comparison to Porto Montenegro and new residential developments in Japan, as well as the possibility of another on the West Coast of the USA (hence Tino's satellite office in Los Angeles).

Nate McBride links this growing responsibility to Tino's overall vision on multiple levels. "Tino can move in and out like a telescope," he says. "Nothing gets missed." James Reginato, however, highlights the versatility. "An international star, Tino is capable of working in any style or country," says the author.

Indeed, Tino's only weakness is buying real estate. Recently, he added an Athens apartment to his list of properties, which include Paris, Gstaad, London, New York, and a house on Hydra. Putting it down to Tino's strong Greek roots, David Mlinaric is not surprised. "He always planned on buying a home there," he says. Louis-Charles de Rémusat, however, cites "lots of new Greek clients."

Today, Tino Zervudachi is well surrounded by his team of business partners in London, Paris, and New York, whom Nat Rothschild describes as "longstanding, polite, and possessing a sense of humor." By many clients, they are viewed as one of the secrets behind Tino's global success. Tino recognizes the uniqueness of his low-profile team. "Since we don't follow social media, nearly all our projects come to us by word of mouth," he says. In his Paris office, Tino singles out Antoine de Sigy for "his high standards and energy," Marie-Astrid Piron for "her eager and efficient curiosity," and Ohm Wittawat Chulsukon for being "detailed, careful and thoughtful." In London, Tino appreciates Jason Roberts's instinct for "focusing on what matters" and Laurence Macadam's "exacting standards and unrelenting seeking for perfection." And in New York, he admires Lucy Singh for defining "decisive and brave." They go back. "Lucy and I began at David's, she understands the importance of every detail," he says. Meanwhile, the driving force of Tino Zervudachi & Associés is steered by practicality, comfort, and fantasy. "Every project is unique because of the alchemy between the client, the property they've chosen, and the location," says the designer.

RETHINKING TRADITION

However grand the circumstances, Tino Zervudachi avoids complication. "In principle, I like rooms to feel calm even if the decoration is heightened," he says. Nevertheless, a traditional room is disciplined by the architecture. "Most classical rooms will have a fireplace that suggests how to arrange the furniture," he explains. Ever respectful, Tino also works with the cornices, moldings, and other architectural details. According to him, "the combination of architecture and location gives the spirit of a room." Traditional rooms need to be reimagined for today's lifestyles. "The client's personality, imagination, and passions have to be enveloped into the house's architecture and history, to create a new story." Often, the layout of the house and furniture will be reorganized, to make the arrangement of the rooms feel less formal. "That tailored element helps create harmony between the client's lifestyle and the classical architecture."

FACING PAGE
The stuccoed hallway is eye-catching thanks to an Italian sunburst mirror (the client's flea-market find), a nineteenth-century marble-topped iron console table, and two art deco plaster sconces. The newly made marble floor was inspired by the St. Regis hotel in New York. "Reimagining this hallway, with stucco walls, and multicolored marble floor brought a glamorous appeal to the plain space," says Tino.

PAGES 20–21
The first-floor-salon walls are hung with a custom-colored silk chinoiserie damask by Prelle; the curtain pelmets and curtain borders are embroidered by Lesage; cushions are made with fabrics from Prelle and Fortuny; and the ceiling's plasterwork restored and repainted in shades of cream and beige. "Green was the safer bet for this room but I encouraged the client to choose yellow," says Tino. "It is so much more magnificent and makes you happy to be there."

BRINGING BACK GRANDEUR, LONDON

This magnificent Belgravia, terraced corner house was acquired from a British institution. "A listed building, it had been used as offices for about eighty years," says the client. In terrible condition, the early nineteenth-century building had Styrofoam false ceilings, fluorescent lighting, and even a stage for presentations in the first-floor drawing room. Describing Tino's approach as "classical with quality," the client admired his work on London's exclusive Mark's Club and chose him for his experience and highly skilled team. "I like what Tino brings to a complex project and this one was," he explains. The brief was to create a lively family home with a contemporary vocabulary within a classical setting. Working with Sam Bentley from his London office, Tino set about restoring the house's former grandeur and forging harmony between the floors. To establish the principal floor's sumptuous double drawing room, Tino reimagined the interior architecture, responding to the original details by adding

dado paneling and designing classical pilasters, installing antique fireplaces, and gilding the existing overdoors. He also created new doors and stripped back the poorly overpainted ceiling, revealing its elegant moldings and repainting them in a sophisticated and complex, though restrained, palette of several colors. "I thought it's a lovely room to read my newspapers, but will I ever use it?" the client admits. Then Covid struck. "I've been up there every day," he says. To create an elegant architectural space leading into the client's daughter's playroom, Tino paneled the newly created corridor, using different tones of off-white paint, and designed a vaulted ceiling. To gain access to the large upper-floor terrace, Tino created the perfect access, an exquisitely trellised garden room. "I wanted it to be French and formal," says the client. Initially, he balked at Tino's bold color scheme. "I thought, 'That's never going to work,'" he recalled. "However, I now think it's genius and wouldn't change it at all."

ABOVE, LEFT
Tino converted the flat roof of the former garage into this neoclassical trellised terrace. He found the eighteenth-century Louis XV marble fountain in Paris.

ABOVE, RIGHT
The curtain's striped silk taffeta is from Antico Setificio Fiorentino and the mosaic floor is inspired by the neo-Greek Villa Kérylos in the South of France.

FACING PAGE
The trellised breakfast room was created as a link from the living room to the exterior terrace and conceals a dumb waiter from the lower-level kitchen for serving meals.

The ground floor's living room combines nineteenth- and twenty-first-century styles. The exceptional range of fabrics include those from Manufacture Royale Bonvallet for the burnt-orange silk-velvet window seats, made by Howard Chairs, and Prelle for the custom-colored curtains, inspired by an antique Turkish design. Tino found the nineteenth-century neo-Egyptian fireplace in Paris, while the specially created rug was inspired by a 1940s Arbus design.

ABOVE
A detail of the dining room's marron glacé taffeta wall, created by Prelle, and a 1940s French bronze uplighter.

RIGHT
A 1940s Venetian glass chandelier, bought in Paris, hangs above the dining-room table that has a set of Tino Zervudachi's art deco-inspired chairs, upholstered in Le Manach fabric. Drawing attention to the soaring ceilings, Tino imagined a labyrinth design, which he commissioned Laurent Chwast to paint in silver leaf onto canvas.

BELOW, LEFT
The client's collection of black and white photographs frame the corridor's newly paneled walls leading into the ground-floor playroom.

BELOW, RIGHT
The powder room's sink is made of Grand Antique marble, one of Tino's favorites, while the Venetian light is from Barovier & Toso.

FACING PAGE
"We decided to make the kitchen into a paneled room to connect it to the more classical spaces adjacent," says Tino. Three shades of gray were used. The 1960s black glass-topped table is teamed with leather chairs designed by Giuliano Cappelletti and a marble geometric-patterned floor.

"TINO HAS A HEIGHTENED SENSE OF LUXURY; IT SURPRISES BY LOOKING EXCLUSIVE, YET RELAXED." BENJAMIN STEINITZ

VAL DE LOIRE FAMILY CHÂTEAU RESTORED, FRANCE

Layered with memories, this sprawling family home—a principally eighteenth-century château, with some earlier seventeenth-century and later nineteenth-century additions, in the Val de Loire—was inherited from the client's grandfather. "It hadn't been touched since the 1950s," she says. "I chose Tino because I felt he would upgrade the house without sacrificing the spirit." Although the brief was to keep the big, rambling country house atmosphere and imply that little had been done, the project actually took three years. "It was a much bigger job than we expected," says the client. "We ended up gutting the entire place." Working with the architect Sébastien Desroches, Tino Zervudachi restructured the entire château by changing floor levels, turning a servants' hall into a kitchen, altering the old stables into a playroom, and converting an old staff wing into more guest rooms, with dressing rooms and bathrooms, demonstrating how the concept of traditional comfort has evolved. Occasionally, Tino encountered pleasant surprises, such as some beautiful eighteenth-century beams hidden behind several layers of later ceilings. He also had to edit the client's grandparents' vast collection of objects and art. "Tino did a fantastic job," says the client. "A real skill, the rooms look like they had always been like that." Local artisans—unused to Tino Zervudachi's exacting standards—caused the occasional setback. However, the ever-tenacious designer succeeded and won praise from the client's family. "Their attitude was, 'You didn't just improve it, you literally made it better than it was,'" she recalls.

BELOW
The exterior of the largely eighteenth-century château has a Directoire façade, which Tino restored, adjusting the roof line and stone cornices and re-opening a blocked up window to enhance its elegance. "The château was originally covered in ivy," says the client.

RIGHT
Robert Longo's charcoal drawing of a knight—nicknamed "the guardian of the château" by Tino—adds a contemporary edge to the antique-filled entrance hall. A nineteenth-century Dutch chandelier hangs above a seventeenth-century scagliola-topped Florentine table, while nineteenth-century cloisonné lamps sit on nineteenth-century side tables. The newly installed floor is a classic French design made of limestone with black cabochons. "We opened up the entrance of the château by knocking down walls that had formed four rooms, in order to create a welcoming, light-filled hallway," says Tino.

PAGES 30–31

"The original fireplace inspired the color of the library's paneling," Tino explains. To achieve that particular green patina, Tino commissioned Laurent Chwast, who used the eighteenth-century *colle de peau de lapin* technique. A pair of Bridgewater sofas by Howard Chairs are upholstered in a Pierre Frey silk velvet, and are in conversation with a nineteenth-century slipper chair in an antique striped linen, as well as a Louis XV bergère in an Andrew Martin fabric. Tino reimagined the room with the natural wood-beamed ceiling to give a sense of history. "When Tino moved an object, drawing, or a piece of furniture, it felt like they were being rediscovered and suddenly getting a new lease of life," says the client. "We sourced this beautiful pink Oushak rug from Beauvais Carpets in New York," adds Tino. "The brave combination of colors feels fresh and warm."

TOP LEFT

Looking out on the garden redesigned by French landscape designer Louis Benech, windows are curtained in a Jean Roze fabric with Indian-inspired embroidered borders designed by Tino and made by Maximiliano Modesti.

BOTTOM LEFT

A bronze owl, named Noor, by Anthon Hoornweg, was bought by the client and sits on the sill of an œil-de-bœuf window. "The bird is the château's protector," observes the client.

FACING PAGE

The drawing room is painted with a layered patina in duck-egg blue color. The columned passage to the front of the house, with its arched windows and central door to the terrace, creates an inviting area for morning reading. The ceiling has been patinated with several layers of paint, creating an aged, "moss-marked" appearance.

FACING PAGE
In the top-floor TV room, the spectacular eighteenth-century oak roof structure is enhanced by Tino's choice of furniture, which includes a pair of vintage Philip Arctander clam chairs, an ottoman upholstered in Le Manach's Vache fabric, a four-seater Jean-Michel Frank-style sofa covered in Holland & Sherry's wool flannel, and a Cindy Calicut striped carpet manufactured by Shyam Ahuja.

BELOW
A Hartley flat-weave striped carpet unifies the hallway leading into the guest rooms; Tino painted borders on the walls and ceiling to define the architectural spaces.

RIGHT
Tino was inspired by a visit to Château de Montgeoffroy thirty years earlier. "I remembered this wonderful vaulted kitchen with faux-stone stucco," he says, which helped reimagine the room. Other details include a La Cornue range, bespoke hood and antique *tomette* tiles.

PAGES 36–37
To add charm and atmosphere to the teenagers' recreation room—formerly the stables—Tino restored the vintage basketweave light fixtures and added a billiard table. He also sourced an antique spiral staircase, bought from a Paris flea market which allows access to newly created guest rooms, and chose a bold color scheme for the painted columns. "Those arches originally defined the horse boxes," he explains.

ANGLO-PARISIAN ELEGANCE, PARIS

When a couple of time-honored clients acquired a light-filled Haussmann apartment overlooking the Seine, the challenge was to entirely transform the apartment into a highly appointed and extremely comfortable Parisian pied-à-terre, as comfortable as a magnificent five-star hotel suite, to house their collection of family furniture. Initially designed by Maison Jansen for the owner's mother, although untouched since the 1960s, it was a considerable undertaking. Tino and his Paris business partner, Antoine de Sigy, collaborated with the architect Laurent Minot to fulfill the brief. Designing a dome in the small, newly created, but windowless entrance hall lends a quiet majesty. Decoratively painted with classical motifs, it crowns the glistening, jeweled walls that have been imagined with large stone-block-sized glass panels in *verre églomisé*. In the salon, however, the walls are paneled in a subdued, classical way and painted with a pale palette that creates balance between objects and space. The couple appreciated Tino's subtle innovations—"He is a magician," enthuses the wife. "I couldn't really work with anyone else, nor could my husband." Their elegant lifestyle was Tino's constant inspiration. Nothing feels random: every object, piece of furniture, and picture has been admirably and exquisitely curated and brought together by Tino's decades-long experience with the clients' exacting standards.

TOP RIGHT
A 1625 portrait of the Infanta Maria Anna of Spain by Gonzal Gonzales hangs above a Louis XVI demi-lune marquetry commode with a collection of the owner's objects, including a head attributed to Bernini. The eighteenth-century Louis XVI wing chair is stamped Etienne Meunier and upholstered in Le Manach's Pékin striped silk.

BOTTOM RIGHT
The study is curtained and walled with Percale Persane fabric by Charles Burger and the whole apartment carpeted with a wool Brussels weave trellised floral pattern. The mahogany writing desk is stamped Georges Jacob.

FACING PAGE
In the newly created entrance hall, a nineteenth-century lantern hangs from an elegantly painted neo-classical dome, painted by Laurent Chwast; walls in *verre églomisé* by Florence Girette. "The idea was to rearrange the space from an awkward, chopped-up hallway to create a celebratory arrival into a slightly magical world," says Tino.

RIGHT
Having stripped the
drawing room back
to the concrete,
Tino imagined a paneled
room without moldings,
painting it in several
shades of green patina
with pink accents and
gilding. "It gives a subtle
structure and picks up
the colors of the
furniture," he says.
The striped curtains
are made of an Antico
Setificio taffeta and
the sofa upholstered in
Gretchen Bellinger's linen
velvet. In front, a 1940s
Jansen coffee table.
Tucked away in the corner
is an unusual bronze
coffer on its stand,
created for the space by
André Dubreuil. On the
back wall hangs a pastel
of Lady Brabourne
by Da Pozzo.

The bedroom walls are lined in gray-blue silk velvet from Antico Setificio, set off by curtains made of Tassinari & Chatel's Bleu de la Reine silk faille. A seventeenth-century portrait by the circle of Van Dyke hangs by the window. The chest, covered in Pasha silk velvet, is designed to elegantly hide a rise-and-fall TV, at the foot of the bed.

FACING PAGE
A seventeenth-century Japanese painted-wood panel hangs above a specially commissioned gilded console table sculpted by Philippe Anthonioz. The colors of the panel are echoed in the selection of textiles, carpet and wall patina.

NEO-RENAISSANCE REVIVED, AUSTRIA

This striking nineteenth-century neo-Renaissance villa in Austria was originally built for a wealthy factory owner. When Tino Zervudachi was asked to restore it, the sumptuous building had been subdivided into apartments many years before. The mansion needed to be revitalized for a young, dynamic couple determined to save it from a developer. Everything was dilapidated and covered with a coat of peeling, gray paint. The project was complicated because of the grand décor and historical importance of the building, requiring Tino to work with the local architectural committee to understand the city's arcane rulings. Tino enriched the color schemes by using wallpapers and textiles and commissioned the fine-painting firm Fontana, to execute his reimagined new colors and restore the elaborate painted plasterwork. He was delighted to discover that there had once been an atrium, in the entrance hall, which he was able to redesign adding new marbleized columns to give the impression they had always been there. When stripping back timber panels in the morning room he also uncovered some original painted-mirror panels. As the project advanced, the local authority understood Tino's integrity and vision, and allowed him to install a newly designed staircase, uniting the reception rooms and the private areas of the house.

BELOW
When Tino discovered this space it had been poorly subdivided and the stained-glass windows boarded up. By opening up the space and restoring the rustication, a real sense of arrival has been created, enhanced by the terra-cotta and black color scheme. The hall is lit with a pair of nineteenth-century oil lamps on columns, while the mosaic floor adds to the composition.

FACING PAGE
In the study, a new color scheme was decided upon, inspired by the yellow-marble fluted columns. The elaborate plaster ceilings needed bringing back to life with a paint scheme that balanced with the enriched interior detailing. Tino selected neoclassical Swedish furniture and a large marble hanging light-fixture, to complement the strong architecture. Silk curtains in Lelièvre's Varese striped silk-taffeta and a bespoke carpet from Gallery Parsua complete the scheme.

PAGES 46–47
To freshen up the heavily detailed living room, Tino selected a palette of ivory and pale blues and then heightened the colors of the paint scheme on the ceiling. The aim was to create a balance between all the different elements in the room. "By harmonizing the colors and introducing a patterned Mauny grisaille wallpaper, which was especially colored for the room, we were able to create the sense that the room had always been this way."

PAGES 48–49
A pair of nineteenth-century Swedish chairs and a pair of faux-marble columns lead into the winter garden—a light and airy room—where the color scheme is inspired by Tino's discovery of some original painted mirrored-glass panels. The blinds are a silk stripe by Antico Setificio and the carpet is an especially commissioned Portuguese needlepoint. A pair of Chinese cloisonné lamps sit on either side of the sofa, which is upholstered in a Colefax and Fowler fabric, with specially made cord trimming.

FACING PAGE
"The plasterwork in the breakfast room was so remarkable and splendid that the palette was kept very simple," says Tino, referring to the restrained gray-and-white color scheme and an elegant set of Swedish chairs, a clothed table, and embroidered tone-on-tone cream silk-damask curtains.

RIGHT
After opening up an atrium, discovered to have previously existed in the upper entrance hall of the piano nobile, Tino created a decorative frieze, marbleized the columns, and fluted the ceiling at the far end of the hall. A neoclassical Aubusson-style rug was commissioned to add color and texture to the architectural room.

CITY PALACE, NEW DELHI

This palace in a neo-1930s style was recently built in Chanakapuri, one of New Delhi's leafy and affluent embassy neighborhoods. When Tino first discovered the property, it was incomplete; although the marble walls were already there, it had strange, illogical design flaws. Tino's first goal was to bring in more light and create a better flow of spaces. This was achieved by removing an unnecessary outdoor staircase and creating new windows. It was clearly a house for entertaining, so Tino aimed to create a smart but casual air on the ground floor. He felt the interiors had to be eclectic, too, reflecting the house's different architectural styles. This was achieved by both designing nearly all of the furniture—custom-made in India, with reference to local traditions and motifs—and marrying it with more contemporary pieces and some antiques. Tino and his Paris business partner, Antoine de Sigy, sourced a highly professional group of artisans to collaborate on the project. Tino designed a striking pair of tree-motif embroidered screens, commissioned from Jean-François Lesage in Madras, which embrace a seating area, and a pair of marble consoles with girandole pier-glasses made by Frozen Music, which accentuates the entrance hall. Gradually, a sense of history was added to the house via the choice of eclectic design styles and the artisans' contributions, Tino's acquisitions, and a simple color palette. Moss green evokes the surrounding garden—a lush, jungle-like exterior—and warm mulberry complements the teak ceiling. Although doing business in India demands patience and organization, the project was all the more exciting because it created the opportunity for Tino to fuse his designs with the local artisans' mastery of different material's.

ABOVE, LEFT
"This carpet was designed to feel like a garden path leading you to a secret destination," says Tino, referring to the entrance hall rug.

ABOVE, RIGHT
Tino designed the Indian art deco-inspired console table and over-mirror with attached torchère in order to bring light and reflective surfaces into the marble-walled hallway.

FACING PAGE
Evoking a neo-1930s palace, a pair of hand-carved solid-marble elephants, weighing three tons each, flank the spectacular entrance of an unusual four-story home. "The house had been half-built," says Tino. "We had to furnish it in an eclectic way in order to enhance the rather unusual architecture, which is a mixture of different styles."

PAGES 54–55
At one end of the sitting room, Tino designed the maharaja-style settee and a pair of screens, exquisitely embroidered by Jean-François Lesage. Inspired by Jean-Michel Frank, Tino imagined the red-stone lamps, made by Frozen Music, which echo the colors of the sofa's striped fabric. The pair of lotus side tables are by Nirvaan Design.

FACING PAGE
"Inspired by traditional Indian motifs and details, we needed to design the furniture and rugs, as there was nothing that we could source for this unusual house that was available in India," explains Tino. "This meant working with talented local artisans, though we were able to purchase some decorative art and objects from local galleries," he continues. The daybed and the sofa are made by Splendour, with bespoke cushions by Lesage, and a bookcase built to Tino Zervudachi design by Frozen Music.

RIGHT
From the salon, a view into the dining room, where the appliqué curtains were inspired by the paneled walls of the Red Fort in Old Delhi. On Viya's bespoke cabinet, there is a gold Shiva and pair of lamps purchased from Vikek Sahni. The Dutch ebony chair came from Chiki Doshi's antiques store in Delhi.

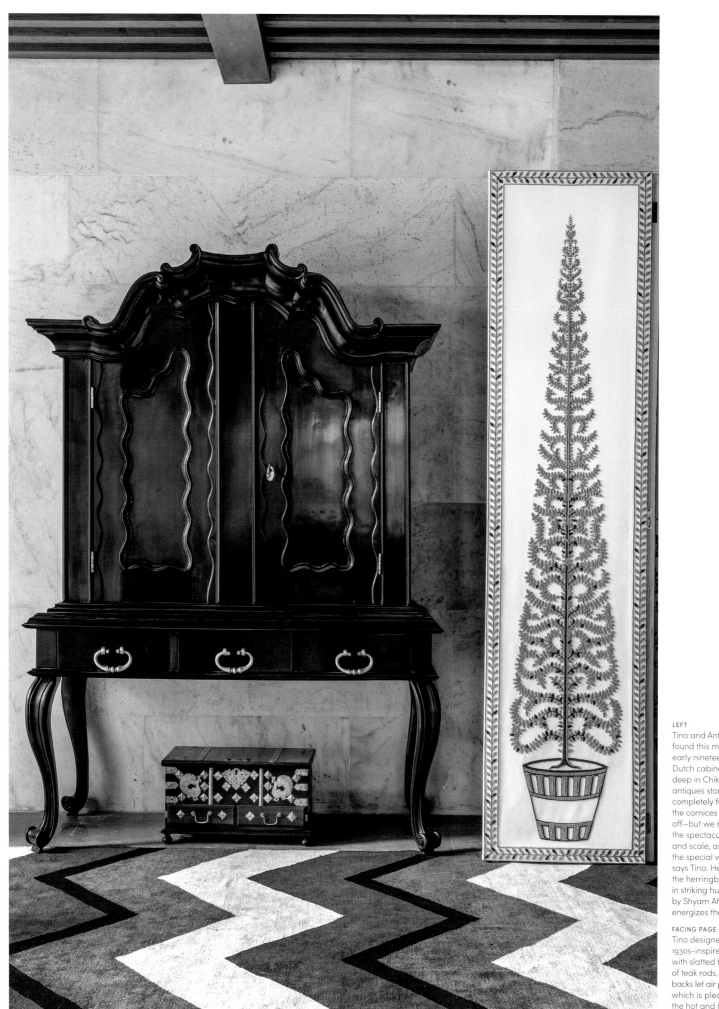

LEFT
Tino and Antoine de Sigy
found this magnificent
early nineteenth-century
Dutch cabinet buried
deep in Chiki Doshi's
antiques store. "It was
completely falling apart—
the cornices had fallen
off—but we recognized
the spectacular carving
and scale, as well as
the special wood,"
says Tino. He designed
the herringbone carpet
in striking hues, woven
by Shyam Ahuja, which
energizes the floors.

FACING PAGE
Tino designed the
1930s-inspired armchairs
with slatted backs made
of teak rods. "The open
backs let air pass through,
which is pleasant in
the hot and humid Indian
climate," he says.

FACING PAGE
When Tino began the
project, an enormous
exterior staircase blocked
the side of the house.
"It would have made the
room completely dark,"
he says. "By removing
the staircase, I was able
to create a series of large
windows that let in light
and allowed a view onto
the jungle-like garden."
Tino designed the
alabaster uplighter
on the column.

ABOVE, LEFT
Reflecting the mixture
of styles, a solid marble
lamp, inspired by
a Jean-Michel Frank
design, sits on a bronze
side-table designed
by Tino, next to an
embroidered cushion
made by Lesage.

ABOVE, RIGHT
Looking into the salon
from the garden terrace.
"It was very invigorating
to work with local
artisans," Tino says.
"By applying ancient
craft techniques to the
designs, they created
new objects and furniture,
a new way of looking
at traditional designs."

WORKING WITH LIGHT

Tino Zervudachi believes in walking through the empty rooms of the houses he has been asked to work on to understand how natural light enters the space. "How it performs in a room is absolutely crucial," he says. "One can be surprised by how light affects spaces and complicates the way you want to arrange furniture or choose colors for a room." Tino views light as an energy that can be manipulated—either released or filtered. "A very dark room often requires bright, bold walls and ceilings, while a sun-filled room sometimes needs softer colors, avoiding the risk of them feeling too harsh." For contemporary interiors that tend to be less symmetrical and less classically organized around windows and fireplaces, this expertise can be particularly transformative."Light nurtures," he says. "When combining furniture and art, it can be used architecturally to define different zones in the room."

FACING PAGE
In the large living room, the painted raffia wall-covering and white linen curtains enhance the general airiness, while the vintage wall lights, purchased in Paris, combined with the 1950s Italian hanging light, give an eclectic feel. "The clients love twentieth-century furniture," says Tino. "Putting in 1950s and 1960s vintage furniture—purchased from Paris, Miami, and New York—gives the house an edge, making it less serious and predictable."

LEFT
In the garden room,
a David Hockney print
sets the casually elegant
tone. A cane sofa by
Bielecky Brothers in
New York is teamed with
a pair of 1950s armchairs
and a boomerang-
shaped coffee table.
The bamboo wall-
covering is by Elitis and
the flat-weave rug is
a Madeline Weinrib
commission.

CARIBBEAN COLORS, BAHAMAS

When the exclusive Lyford Cay Club—a gated community developed in the 1960s—decided to build four villas in the marina, one was snapped up by a couple who had been clients of Tino's for many years. "The marina is where life happens in the club," says the husband. "And because we love boating, it seemed like a great idea." Tino was assisted by his long-term collaborator, Lucy Singh, and the exterior architecture was designed by Kiko Sanchez; the villa's exterior had to be compatible with the rest of the development. "We handed the interiors over to Tino and made huge changes in the floorplan," says the wife. The traditional spaces were made less formal, to suit the clients' bustling, casual lifestyle. Tino enhanced the long hallway with oversized floor tiles and mirrored recesses opposite the windows. He made a large, open-plan kitchen, introduced a bar, and turned a staff room into a guest suite. Everything he did interacted with the owners' yacht, another Tino Zervudachi & Associés (TZA) design project, which is moored in front of the villa. The design of the interior is enhanced by a collection of 1950s and 60s furniture, purchased for the home, with a slight influence from Babe Paley, one of Lyford Cay's historically glamorous residents. The choice of colors was Caribbean bright. "Tino said, 'Be bold, don't hold back,'" recalls the wife. To create a dramatic effect in the hallway, Tino chose a vibrant wallpaper, giving the impression of strolling along a lemon grove. "The whole house stems from that lovely hallway, which was Tino's idea," says the husband. The wife describes the property as a piece of paradise: "You arrive and relax."

"TINO HAS SUCH FLAIR AND SUCH A GREAT IMAGINATION FOR ALL THE DETAIL, YET GETS THE OVERALL SCHEME," SAYS THE CLIENT

ABOVE, LEFT
In the master bedroom, a close-up shows off Mirth Studio's painted wooden floor tiles.

ABOVE, RIGHT
Harvey Probber's vintage chest of drawers is married with Jens Risom's walnut lounge chair, c. 1942.

LEFT
In the hallway, a close-up highlights one of the French feather-shaped glass and bronze sconces. Designed by Gino Sarfatti, they were manufactured by Arteluce in Milan in the 1940s.

FACING PAGE
Inspired by Studio Four's Grove Citron wallpaper, Tino decided to create the lemon-grove hallway. "The idea was to make this circulation space into a celebration of the outside," Tino says.

PAGES 68–69
In the kitchen, which leads into a back pantry and bar, Tino designed 1950s-style cabinetry. Features include sliding glass doors for the upper cabinets and round-edged detailing for the overlay lower-cabinet doors, complete with boat-cleat handles. "This is the type of kitchen that one normally tears out," he says. "It was fun to design and make it spanking new." The Tulip table and chairs are by Saarinen, and the wallpaper is by Studio Four. The light in the bar is a 1960s Italian brass pendant fixture with a pale amber and white spherical glass globe.

WEST VILLAGE TOWNHOUSE, NEW YORK

This small, New York West Village townhouse once belonged to a former gameshow host and even had a puppet theater in the yard. When Tino's client bought the property, it had been gutted and was nothing but an empty shell. Being in Manhattan's historical district, it became a long and extremely complicated project. As is his way, Tino Zervudachi set about working on designs that would add light to the dark, pokey property by staggering the back of the building and by imagining breathtaking, double-height interior spaces, creating unexpected volumes in relation to the small historical façade. Since the brief was to make it warm and inviting, Tino and the client selected a surprising choice of contemporary timber paneling, which adds refinement and elegance throughout. The staircase crisscrosses the house to connect the open spaces, while the cinema in the basement was designed to be womb-like, with an amoeba-shaped, indirectly lit ceiling. Tino made the small, triangular basement-garden look expansive and jungle-like by mirroring one wall and filling it with plants. Throughout the design metamorphosis of this seemingly tiny house, Tino aimed for the dramatic, understanding that an extraordinary space can make any social occasion.

BELOW, LEFT
In the double-height living room, the dining table from Harris Rubin lies in front of the newly created French doors and garden. Tino created all the house's spectacular volumes. "When I first walked in the front door there was nothing here, just a deep well to the basement," he recalls. "All that remained was the street façade and the side walls."

BELOW, RIGHT
A detail of the wooden staircase that leads into the master bedroom, with an elegant lacquered mirror, hanging over a 1960s glass console.

FACING PAGE
The double-height living room with a mix of styles of furniture including Hans J Wegner's Papa Bear chair and Vladimir Kagan's credenza. The light fixture is on an electrically operated telescopic rod to avoid blocking the film projector and screen that drops down in front of the fireplace. "A double-height room can sometimes be a bit cold," says Tino. "So polished timber walls warm it up, whilst the staircase gives a theatrical dimension."

PAGES 72–73
Tino's goal was to make the living room into a light-filled, masculine, downtown lair. Sumptuous details include cashmere curtains from Rogers & Goffigon, a bespoke sectional sofa covered in an abstract gray-and-white printed silk-velvet by Castel, a pair of A. Rudin armchairs, and Lucca & Co.'s long coffee table with seagrass stone top. Tino sourced a 1940s hammered-iron fireplace, which inspires the curves of the room, while light pouring in from the skylight is reflected in the leather-framed mirror.

BELOW
Tino designed the
diner-like banquette
as a cozy kitchen corner,
by selecting Jean Prouvé's
Japanese-style oak and
metal chairs, Bonderup
& Thorup's vintage
pendant light, and a
George Nelson clock.

FACING PAGE
An amoeba-like ceiling
recess incorporating
indirect lighting adds
character to the newly
created cinema. The
sofa-like chaises longues
by B&B Italia upholstered
in gray-patterned velvet,
along with Holland &
Sherry's deep-blue velvet
walls and Rug Art's
peacock-blue-patterned
carpet, lend an air of
modern luxury. The wall
sconces are from Bernd
Goeckler, Reggiani
edition, 1969.

FACING PAGE
Since light pours into the master bedroom through the newly created skylight, it is also fitted with electric blackout blinds. Poul Henningsen's iconic Artichoke light, manufactured by Louis Poulsen, hangs above a Boogi wool-and-silk carpet made by Rug Art in New York. A 1946 swing-arm floor lamp by Arredoluce, and a 1950s Ramos Eggshell chair from Alan Moss complete the room.

RIGHT
For the bedroom's sitting area, Tino chose two Kalos swivel chairs, upholstered in Holland & Sherry wool satin that contrast with the dark walls. The 1950s Cristal Arte mirror is from Bernd Goeckler Antiques. "We used a lot of Italian-designed furniture because it is so strong and it manages to be both masculine and playful."

BELOW
By installing a big dormer window, Tino was able to make a spectacular bathroom/dressing room with a freestanding bath and Wolf Gordon raffia-covered cupboards that line the walls. A Retro Modern lamp sits on a 1950s Jansen side table.

RIGHT
Characteristic of Tino's
signature style, a console
table sculpted by
Manuela Zervudachi
and a pair of Frank Gehry
chairs greet guests
in the entrance hall.

PAGES 80–81
"To keep the living
room feeling simple,
we used a plain palette,
of blue and white," Tino
explains. Nevertheless,
the Brunschwig fabric
energizes the room.
The wood-grain pattern
on the Jean-Michel
Frank-inspired sofa
from Anthony Lawrence-
Belfair vibrates, and
the client's own chairs
are covered in Nobilis
Mazurka fabric to add
a geometric twist. The
custom-made carpet
by Stark is viewed under
Manuela Zervudachi's
glass-topped bronze
coffee table.

MID-CENTURY
MODERNIZED, LONG ISLAND

This country house was acquired by a discerning New York
couple interested in twentieth-century art. The sprawling
mid-century house with neoclassical hints had an irrational
layout as it had grown over the years to accommodate
the previous owner's changing family situation. Although
set in an extraordinary location overlooking the north shore
of Long Island Sound, this hodgepodge of styles was
discordant. Tino Zervudachi, with the architect Agatha
Habjan, decided to simplify and clarify the house's conflicting
styles to make it more contemporary. Ceilings were raised
in the living room and entrance hall, making spectacular
spaces, while a bay window became a feature when
enlarged to create a seating area looking to the views. It was
a cellular house with a central pavilion and corridors leading
to other wings, so Habjan and Zervudachi rearranged the
spaces to suit the new owners' needs. The symmetrical
galleries now serve the guest rooms, with a wing for their
adult sons at one end, and the other side leading to an open
and minimalist kitchen, which is located between the family
dining space and the formal dining room. The previous
conflicting styles of the house were incoherent, with chintzy
curtains and flouncy valances on large, modern windows,
which felt wrong; fitting in with his client's restrained taste,
Tino's approach was to create something more sophisticated
and contemporary, relying on graphic and geometric textiles,
and rugs with simple, classic silhouettes. The request for a
bar provided the opportunity to work with a material made
from recycled bottles and the client's interest in art allowed
him to commission newly designed pieces, such as a
Manuela Zervudachi console for the entrance hall and
bronze coffee table for the living room.

FACING PAGE
"The back of the bar
and top is made out of
a material created from
recycled bottles and
backlit, which creates
an amazing effect," says
Tino. To the right, the
cool, cinematic hallway
leads to the bedrooms.

BELOW
Through the stylish
hallway—formed with
broad walnut panels—
can be seen the garden
and courtyard, created
by landscape designer
Reed Hilderbrand.

PAGES 84–85
A view through
the contemporary
kitchen—exemplified
by its seamless
Valcucine glass-fronted
cabinetry—into the
dining room towards
a painting by Hadieh
Shafie, which appears
like a window onto
another space.

"TINO KNEW WHERE I WAS COMING FROM AND WOULD ALWAYS
BE GRACIOUS ABOUT MY CHOICES. WHAT'S REFRESHING IS THAT HE'S
INCREDIBLY TALENTED BUT DOESN'T TAKE HIMSELF SERIOUSLY," SAYS THE CLIENT

ZEN ELEGANCE, TOKYO

Emanating calm and tranquility, this oasis-like house is a few minutes away from one of Tokyo's busiest shopping streets. The property on which the new house stands had been a parking lot with two very poorly built, prefab houses on it. The potential lay in the large size of constructible land, highly unusual for the city. Tino wrote to the revered architect Kengo Kuma and explained that his client was fascinated by Japanese culture. Wood/Berg—Kuma's name for the project—became one of his first private projects for a European client. It resulted in a seven-story building made of steel, clad in glass and wood, and incorporating a slatted screening system blending it into the architectural fabric of the city, while ensuring privacy from the street. Familiar with the long-standing client's needs, Tino carefully determined the spaces required and focused on the necessary atmosphere: a calm and elegant home with European comfort and a harmonious Japanese feel.

Since furniture is not part of traditional local culture, Tino designed everything, along with his London-based partner, Laurence Macadam, and had the pieces executed by T.C.K.W., artisans esteemed for their expertise in traditional Japanese crafts. One challenge was how to address the unusual sloping walls and windows, which created tremendous complication with regards to window treatments. To filter light, Tino ended up commissioning electric blinds with Japanese painted-motifs that both rose up from the floor and descended from the ceiling. To divide the salon from the dining area, Tino installed a mobile eight-panel bamboo screen rather than a solid wall, so that light could pass through from one side of the room to the other. To enhance the Zen aesthetic, yet make it feel inviting and warm, Japanese Washi rice paper covers the walls, while a soft, natural palette was achieved by the selection of natural woods and stone throughout.

ABOVE
Kengo Kuma's wall of signature wood-louvered panels are designed to filter and mold light. "The building suddenly appears quite unexpectedly off a side street," he describes.

FACING PAGE
Every piece of furniture in this tranquil and comfortable double-height living room was designed by Tino and his London business partner Laurence Macadam and custom-made in Tokyo by T.C.K.W.'s artisans.

FACING PAGE
The lengthy living room is bathed in an extraordinary light, received from front and back. Since the space doubles as a dining area, Tino screened off the dining table with natural-fiber panels. "Created with Sudare bamboo, the panels were made in such a way that they could be tilted to open up the two spaces", he says.

RIGHT
On the other side of the living room, Tino commissioned the dining room's contemporary mobile from Hirotoshi Sawada, a Japanese sculptor, that can be seen through the slatted panels.

TOP LEFT
Following the client's request for a swimming pool, Kuma and Tino joined forces to create an enigmatic 45 foot (13.7-meter) lap pool. "As it is in the second basement, we wanted to evoke this dark, womb-like, reassuring and restful feeling," Tino says. This was achieved by concealing recessed mood-lighting in the ceiling and walls, using travertine Navona stone for the floors and walls and creating the water's blue color via underwater side-lighting. All the teak and stainless-steel furniture is designed by Thailand-based Kenkoon.

BOTTOM LEFT
The hinoki-wood basin in the master bathroom demonstrates Kuma's revered skill with wood.

FACING PAGE
The master bedroom, observed from the roof, has spectacular views and is secluded from the rest of the house. "It was both exciting and invigorating to work with someone as talented as Kuma," Tino says.

UPPER EAST SIDE
PIED-À-TERRE, NEW YORK

Due to a growing American clientele, Tino Zervudachi wanted a New York pied-à-terre where he could rest quietly, surrounded by his own art and belongings, when in town for his projects. In 2008 he found an apartment in the former Barbizon Hotel for Women (1927). Known for its glamorous residents, the establishment was being converted into condominiums. Tino was sold on the location and charmed by the classic Manhattan views. The apartment faces all cardinal points, boasting windows to the ceiling, with low windowsills that receive the light differently throughout the day. When the sun sets, the ambiance becomes otherworldly. After acquiring a further unit from one of the original Barbizon tenants in 2018, Tino was able to fuse them both by working with the architect Libe Camarena. Tino chose Japanese wallpapers for the walls, as a backdrop to enhance his art collection, and in the corridor, two large walls were mirrored to open and widen the space. For the furnishings he decided to mix mid-century modern new purchases with some favorites from former homes, along with contemporary one-off pieces, often commissioned from friends. The selection is eclectic, and the emotional impact is strong. The tranquil apartment gives the sensation of floating amongst the neighboring towers. It is not too far from the street, yet high enough to feel protected. In a chaotic and frantic city, the apartment has become Tino Zervudachi's welcome refuge.

LEFT
In Tino's Manhattan entrance hall, the walls are covered in dark green Japanese rice-paper from Kamism in Tokyo. The steel-based table with an antique-marble top is designed by Gerald Bland, and the set of four red lacquered Bankshuhl chairs are by Willy Guhl for Stendig. On the walls, a striking abstract painting by Noémie Rocher contrasts with Christopher Winter's *Ghost Training* painting.

RIGHT
Looking down the hallway, covered with specially commissioned Japanese "splash" rice-paper panels, Matthew Day Jackson's multimedia collage of flowers hangs prominently, picking up the colors of Thomas Schute's pink-and-green painting in the entry.

PAGES 94–95
To create a calming atmosphere in the library end of the living room, Tino chose a monochromatic scheme, hence the upholstery is the same color as the Japanese wallpaper and bookcase. "I wanted it to feel far away from the hurly-burly of New York outside," he says. Embroidered giraffe-motif cushions are combined with silk ones by Yastik.

BELOW, LEFT
In the study, a graphic acrylic by British artist Christopher Winter hangs above a Philippe Anthonioz bronze and glass desk and a pair of 1910 Swedish chairs with neoclassical marquetry backs.

BELOW, RIGHT
Kiki Smith's owl sculpture perches above a Richard Long painting, with a 1940s Robsjohn-Gibbings slipper chair underneath. A small black Constellation table with laminated ash legs, by Edward Wormley for Dunbar, was purchased from Lobel Modern in New York.

FACING PAGE
In the living room, an African mask and an astonishing abstract work by Olafur Eliasson, created with ice from a glacier, are positioned by the curved Thomas O'Brien banquette.

PAGES 98–99
In Tino's corner bedroom—which boasts four windows—a landscape by Gregory Johnston hangs above the bed. A circular color study by the same artist rests between two windows and is set off by the Kamism wallpaper from Tokyo, which matches the indigo-cloth bedcover. "I wanted a cool and restful bedroom," says Tino.

"TINO IS A COLLECTOR AND SOMEONE WHO REALLY LOVES ART. I ADMIRE THE WAY THAT HE CAN VIEW EXHIBITIONS, CAREFULLY LOOK, AND GET INVOLVED." THADDAEUS ROPAC

LIVING
WITH COLOR

Tino Zervudachi is especially sought out for his sensual and playful way with color. He is one of the many interior designers who actively encourage it when clients are open to it. "Color leads to individuality and both energizes and warms up a room," he enthuses. Recognizing the fear factor—"People can be scared of choosing the wrong palette"—Tino understands today's trend for bland, monochrome interiors, but discourages it when he feels that color will add depth. "Color does not have to be forceful and bright," he reasons. "It can be subtle with delicate tones. Color can also be disciplined via a refined choice of textiles, rugs, and upholstery to create harmony." Since color is deeply personal, there are no rules. "Outrageous colors can feel great for some people," Tino states. There again, he suggests a layering of other elements in the room. "As always, it's about achieving a balance," he says.

FACING PAGE
To lend a graphic and dynamic sharpness, Tino and his client chose Maharam fabric for custom-made Roman blinds, which flank an eighteenth-century French clock, from the client's collection. The oak chairs by Patricia Urquiola are covered in suede in different colors, and face each other across the fluted, plaster table from John Rosselli.

LEFT
Using the complementary colors of yellow and purple for the entrance hall, Tino selected strong graphic wallpaper from Jupiter 10's Vienna collection, and designed flush, purple-lacquered doors, used throughout the whole apartment. Cove lighting in the ceiling is amplified by a yellow stripe that picks up Christian Astuguevieille's Moisson Senegal chair, adding a touch of exoticism.

FACING PAGE
Nelly Munthe's exuberant rug unifies artwork, furniture, and textiles, which include a Pierre Frey embroidered fabric on a love seat and the Anthony Lawrence-Belfair sofa, upholstered in Manuel Canovas's red velvet for Bandol.

MANHATTAN KALEIDOSCOPE, NEW YORK

Reflecting the busy, quintessential atmosphere of the Upper East Side, this pied-à-terre was acquired by a European art collector. She wanted a bright and cheerful home when visiting her Manhattan-based family. Initially, the apartment resembled a dull, boxy set of rooms, untouched for many decades, which needed transforming into a vibrant, modern space. Working alongside the New York-based architect Pietro Cicognani, a total back-to-the-concrete renovation was decided upon.

After taking down all the false ceilings, they put in new false beams of varying widths to reestablish a logical, graphic arrangement to balance with the existing structural beams. Tino painted the ceilings in different colors to create visual interest, adding contrasting colored lines of paint to create the effect of architectural cornices. The client was closely

involved in the overall process of the color schemes; dynamic and knowledgeable, she is an adventurous art collector who truly relishes a bold palette. The brief was to dream up a comfortable place that mixed some of her family furniture and objets d'art with fun, contemporary pieces that she had recently bought. Thanks to their experience together on previous projects, she and Tino were on the same wavelength and were able to bounce ideas back and forth, spending considerable time composing the jewel-toned color schemes and the interior architecture to make the space flow easily. When viewed from the den, the brilliant lemon-yellow kitchen is designed to resemble a cabinet of curiosities. The result is very different from her other homes; the client views her Manhattan pied-à-terre as a joyful break from tradition.

PAGES 104–5
"My client's curious nature and confident taste allows a pair of beaded African thrones to be combined with the finest eighteenth-century French furniture, as shown by the commode behind," says Tino.

ABOVE AND FACING PAGE
In the den, the client's accumulated collection of African textiles was made into cushions that offer a riot of color and tie in with the bright yellow of the kitchen, seen through the doorway. "Working closely with the client and architect Pietro Cicognani, we wanted to create a playful and striking palette of colors to enhance the small spaces."

A TRAVELER'S EYE, LONDON

A South American collector with a discerning eye acquired a large nineteenth-century London house that had been disfigured by previous owners with ugly detailing, inappropriate moldings, and a poor layout. Tino and his client wanted to create an elegant and appropriate architectural scheme, to produce a cosmopolitan environment that enhanced the client's exceptional book and art collection reflecting her passion for travel. She was both exacting and confident about her perception of interiors, wanting a controlled and calm setting, but giving rein to her exotic sense of style and color. Tino Zervudachi, working with his London team, Joanna Szczygiel, Constantin Cantacuzene, and Laurence Macadam, called on the architect Chris Mitchell. They initially thought that they might try to salvage certain elements of the previous design, but they ended up by deciding to gut the entire house in order to achieve the right proportions. Every room had to be redesigned, and Tino incorporated a new architectural language. The house had the advantage of having windows on three sides, filling it with light. Since the client entertains in a relaxed manner, Tino imagined an elegant downstairs kitchen, which required lowering the floor, and the former kitchen was then turned into a large, garden-level dining room that spills out onto the patio, leading into a garden designed by the acclaimed landscape architect Libby Russell. The ground floor is more formal in tone and includes a drawing room and library. The calm elegance of these apparently simple rooms belies a highly precise management of the spaces and furniture arrangements. The result is an exotic yet controlled environment, which houses a traveler's extremely varied and cultivated tastes, from nineteenth-century European painting to Asian aboriginal art.

LEFT
In the drawing room, a sofa, with cushions made from exotic antique silks collected over years, is upholstered in Alton Brooke's antique gold silk-velvet. A pair of cream-silk-covered Louis XVI bergère fauteuils flank the ancient Roman marble table, on which stands an Indonesian effigy.

RIGHT
Highlighting the exotic
eclecticism in the two
rooms, the walls are kept
deceptively simple, with
a subtle plaster finish,
and the parquet floors
covered with simple
hemp and jute
custom-made matting
rugs. The superb pair
of eighteenth-century
Waterford crystal
chandeliers hang above
two Napoleon III slipper
chairs and the remarkable
coffee table made from
a second-century Roman
fountain that rests on
a bronze base, sculpted
by Bruno Romeda. "The
controlled color palette
gives harmony to the
client's collection of
art from exotic places
and eighteenth- and
nineteenth-century
gilded furniture,"
says Tino.

LEFT
In the library, Tino
took the owner's book
collection as his cue
for the design of the
bookcases and coffered
ceiling. The bookcase
ladder is upholstered
in pigskin by Poulain in
Paris. The nineteenth-
century French chair is
covered in Jim Thompson
fabric, and sits next
to a nineteenth-century
gilded wooden
allegorical sculpture,
stretched out in front of
the marble fireplace.

FACING PAGE
In the library's bay
window an inviting
built-in buttoned
banquette sits beneath
Lilou Marquand's Chicks
blinds. It is upholstered
in Sabina Fay Braxton's
teal-blue velvet with
cushions made from
antique textiles—
collected by the client on
her travels—and a pair of
Syrian mother-of-pearl
tables stand in front.

PAGE 115
By lowering the floor, Tino turned the former kitchen into an elegant dining room with a tropical atmosphere. Curtains are made of embroidered fabric from Tissus d'Hélène; a marble-topped table with a bronze base adds to the indoor-outdoor feel. The client added a set of nineteenth-century Sri Lankan carved Macassar-ebony chairs. "The client and I worked hand in hand on the spaces, and I followed her lead in terms of atmosphere," Tino says.

LEFT
The lower-ground kitchen keeps fresh with dark green enameled lava stone backsplash, black and white chequerboard tiled floor and handwoven-rattan Claude Cultot chairs.

FACING PAGE
A mid-century Italian milky-glass and bronze light hangs by the Tino Zervudachi-designed wrought-iron balustrade made by Schmidt & Cie., with a herringbone runner on the stairs.

PAGE 114
The roof terrace that leads off from the living room creates the space for the dining room below, which leads out to the garden dining area. "We liked the idea of trellis walls for the patio, to create a structured architectural setting," says Tino. Libby Russell designed the garden and a beautiful planting scheme of bleeding heart, roses, and clematis, to create a romantic woodland feel, drawing one's eye into the back of the garden, where a Gothic wooden pavilion stands, used as a playhouse by the client's grandchildren.

FACING PAGE
To add masculine
glamour, the entire
bathroom was clad
in marble, and includes
a glassed-in steam
shower and marble tub.

BELOW, LEFT
An elegant, nineteenth-
century pewter-topped
table stands in front
of the window.

BELOW, RIGHT
In the spacious,
onyx-clad master
bathroom, Tino, with
his London team, created
a vaulted ceiling and
designed the 1930s-style
vanity based on images
the client had selected
for inspiration.

COLOR AND FORM, TORONTO

When looking to move downtown from a more formal residential neighborhood, some former clients called on Tino Zervudachi again to reimagine and create something special in a terraced townhouse in central Toronto. To their mind, the new house was wonderfully convenient and had space to create a garden, though it was in very poor condition. Tino's directives were to transform the house into a luxurious two-bedroom home where the couple could entertain, as well as incorporate their furniture and art collection, which ranges from seventeenth-century Chinese ceramics to a twentieth-century European and North American sculpture, and Canadian Inuit art. The house, in need of complete rearrangement of the spaces, was reconceived, and Tino, working with architect Adam Smuszkowicz, literally had to rethink the entire five floors. The house needed to be extended on the ground floor, in order to install a large kitchen and dining room; and on the first floor to create the large living room. They also designed a sweeping staircase placed in the center of the building. The clients wanted color and hoped for something that was creative, uplifting, and stylish. Tino took tremendous inspiration from their paintings and varied collection that includes Calder, Giacometti, and modern Canadian artists. For instance, in the living room, Tino designed a rug inspired by a Japanese kimono silk, woven by Galerie Diurne in Tibet, and upholstered a pair of Louis XV armchairs in an eye-catching blue silk velvet. He also encouraged the clients to bring in pieces from a former house he had made for them, such as the bespoke dining table designed by David Linley for their country estate outside Toronto, and Philippe Anthonioz's bronze lanterns.

FACING PAGE
Tino designed the living room's carpet, inspired by an eighteenth-century kimono. "I wanted to bring all the different colors of the room together and create movement in order to echo the curves in the furniture," he says.

RIGHT
To achieve the stairway's vibrant patina—in parrot-green—many different layers of paint were applied by a painting specialist. Meanwhile, the combination of Philippe Anthonioz's wrought-iron sculpted lantern and the black-and-marble, diamond-patterned floor adds a stylish punch, alongside the glass and bronze Tino Zervudachi-designed balustrade.

ABOVE
At one end of the living room, the silk twill-covered walls enhance the feeling of comfort and act as a restrained background to the multicolored silk cushions on the sofas. A black and white photo by Scott McFarland hangs above the sofa and in front a Diego Giacometti coffee table is surrounded by a pair of armchairs and Louis XVI fauteuils.

FACING PAGE

In the dining room, the Louis XVI chairs with seat squabs covered in Edmond Petit's velour Palerme. The green silk blinds are made from an Antico Setificio specially colored weave, with borders embroidered by Tree of Life, that contrast elegantly with the gouache by Alexander Calder.

PAGES 124–25

Tino's client desired a house that felt bright and cheerful, to contrast with Toronto's grey and harsh winters. A red dining room was chosen, picking up the red from the eighteenth-century Chinese cabinet just outside, and using red details for the blinds and carpeting up the stairs in the stair hall. Silver leaf on the ceiling of the dining room was applied in a checkered pattern to create a subtle glimmer that reflects light. The red silk brocatelle blinds contrast with the black Astrakhan velvet by Colony, which covers the Louis XVI fauteuils.

LEFT
In the entrance hall Canadian art hangs above an eighteenth-century Canadian commode which stands in a recess of the newly created oval room, with reeded plaster walls and a black and white marble floor.

FACING PAGE
The house was extended to create the space for the new kitchen, including a glass-roofed bay window that houses the breakfast table, and quartz backlit backsplashes bringing light onto the countertops on the other side of the kitchen.

A COLLECTOR'S COUNTRY HOME, NEW ENGLAND

Nestled in a lush New England landscape, this traditionally styled famer's house was built from the ground up, although it seems to have existed for centuries. It was conceived for a client who was enchanted with Tino's previous input in the renovation of one of her family homes, and who had purchased a piece of land that included the remains of ancient stone walls built by early settlers. She wanted a typical stone farmhouse, like one that might have once belonged to a prosperous farmer. "It was my dream house and a huge project," says the client. "It had to look old; accurate but not cheesy." Tino suggested hiring Ferguson & Shamamian, with whom he had worked before, along with his longtime, close friend, the landscape designer Miranda Brooks for this monumental task. The existing house was poorly located on the land, so he and Brooks suggested building the house at the top of the plot, to take maximum advantage of the sweeping views of the lower wetlands, where a small lake was created. "Miranda also found a young stonemason, Nicholas Stauder from Northstone Landscaping, who did an outstanding job,"

notes the client. "We almost only used rocks from the land. Energetically that suits me." Tino was searching for authenticity and nursed fears that the house would feel new and unpatinated. Fortunately, with intellectual and creative collaboration between the whole team and the client, attention to every detail in the project led to a remarkable, seamless result. "One of my pet peeves is houses that are a historical hodge-podge," she says. Antique floors and fireplaces, sourced by Tino, were shipped over from Europe, as well as her own family's ancestral furniture. Tino worked with Oscar Shamamian and Andrew Oyen, from Ferguson & Shamamian, for many months on getting the details accurate inside and out. Meanwhile, the layered interior decoration, while deceptively simple, includes vibrant colors and unusual solutions. Hence the paneled walls in the hallway, lacquered in a deep, glossy Corsican blue—an elegant background for the stalwart Jacobean furniture—and the bright blue lacquered pantry. The client's desire for a home that had grown from layers of family history and travels was beautifully realized.

PAGES 130–31
In the drawing room, an eighteenth-century Irish crystal chandelier hangs over a 1950s elm and oak desk by Frits Henningsen, along with an Austrian Biedermeier walnut armchair upholstered in Carolina Irving velvet fabric. The corkscrew, white-plaster lamp base is from Liz O'Brien and the walls are covered in a custom-*gaufraged* French linen from Pierre Frey. "I wanted the house to feel that it had grown from travels," says the client. "There is a mixture of old furniture, which belonged to my family, and new, with a layer of art." The bronze and marble side tables are signed Maison Saridis and designed by Robsjohn-Gibbings, circa 1960. For the client's exceptional Dupré-Lafon cabinets, Tino designed stands, made by Christian Mussy, to put them at the right height between the windows.

LEFT
The stylish chocolate-brown lacquered bar was created to feel warm and welcoming. "It is special," says Andrew Oyen. "Like something you'd find in London or Paris. Tino nicknamed it, 'Cindy's bar,' after one of our architects who worked on it with him." The bar is upholstered in a dark brown leather with nailing around the panel edges.

FACING PAGE
In the drawing room's dining area, a 1940s mahogany table along with oak and leather dining chairs by Kaare Klint all rest on a Wheel of Life rug, designed by Tino, woven in Tibet, and ordered from Galerie Diurne. "The drawing room is the house's principal room, and includes the dining room and two sitting areas in it," says Tino. "The idea being that the huge light-filled room would be like a 'light box' to view the property beyond from."

"TINO WOULD ENCOURAGE ALL MY IDEAS, PARTICULARLY THE MORE UNUSUAL THOUGHTS, SUCH AS CREATING A DAYBED IN THE LIBRARY BOW WINDOW, OR A CLASSICAL OUTDOOR FIREPLACE BY THE SWIMMING POOL," **SAYS THE CLIENT**

FACING PAGE
The pool house is tucked away by the foot of a newly made wall to conceal from the house. A pair of Michael Taylor wood-framed sofas converse over two 1960s coffee tables purchased in Paris and a 1950s rattan chair. The monumental flagstones with grassy joints give a feeling of always having been there.

ABOVE
The library has pale-oak bookcases and a barrel-vaulted ceiling with elegantly painted strapping motif designed by Tino. "We bought an 1870s Axminster carpet with very strong colors, which inspired the selection of textiles for the room," says Tino.

FACING PAGE
In the kitchen, Tino designed vegetal and animal-themed micro-mosaic panels, which form the kitchen's backsplash, made by Frozen Music in Jaipur. "Tino came up with this idea of having whimsical sayings in French and Latin about food and drink," says the client. "Really special and unusual, it has fruits, vegetables, and animals and resembles something from a villa in Pompeii."

RIGHT
In the butler's pantry, the cabinetry is lacquered in high-gloss peacock blue. The design of the cabinets is inspired by an antique Regency mahogany cabinet found by Tino in Amsterdam. "This is a buffer space between the drawing room and the kitchen," he says. "So we wanted it to be a beautiful transition room to view from the living room and to walk through to the kitchen."

FACING PAGE
In the master dressing room, in order to close the open closets requested by the client, Tino designed electronically operated, backlit blinds that roll up at the press of a button. He imagined them ike Japanese screens , and had them painted in Paris to create a scenographic garden.

BELOW, LEFT
Tino designed the elevator to look like the exterior of a vintage trunk, "with waxed canvas walls, timber battens, and brass nails," he says.

BELOW, RIGHT
In a Morocco-inspired guest bathroom, Tino used Zellige tiles for the walls, and designed the closet as an archway with wood fretwork made in Morocco for the doors.

LEFT
Planet 9, a 240-foot
(73.2-meter) steel-hulled
expedition yacht, lying
resplendent in Brooklyn
Marina. Tino's brief was
to create *Planet 9*'s bold
interior to be masculine
and luxurious.

PAGES 142–43
The indoor/outdoor
living room's walls are
paneled in polished teak.
A glass-topped table
with polished-steel base,
designed for the space
by Tino, and director's
chairs by Glyn Peter
Machin, create the dining
area. In the foreground
outside is an elegant,
expanding dining table
made by Christian
Mussy. "When thinking
about this room,
I was looking to create
a space that enhanced
the nautical lifestyle,
making an internal space
feel as if it were part
of the exterior and
celebrating the beauty
of the sea."

BOLD NAUTICAL DESIGN, *PLANET 9*

Measuring a staggering 240 feet (73.2 meters), *Planet 9*
is an explorer yacht that was built by Admiral Yachts in Italy.
Destined for Jules Verne-type adventure, the vast vessel is
purposed for long-distance cruising and extreme weather—
the hull is ice-classed—and comes with a helicopter, hangar,
and helipad. The British owner and longtime client explains,
"Tino has an ease with people and you're not wasting time."
Tino's brief was that *Planet 9* had to be extremely
comfortable, but masculine and streamlined. The master
stateroom is, unusually, located on a lower deck, for quiet
and more stability, and fitted out with exotic woods and
textiles. Since the guest deck has its own beach club at
the stern of the boat, Tino made a feature of the long guest
stateroom corridor by employing a subtle gradation of
the same fabric for the walls, but darker at the center
of the vessel and lighter toward the stern. Each cabin boasts
a different-colored leather door, to help guests locate their
quarters, and is clad in varying woods such as American elm,
tropical olive wood, and Brazilian wacapou. In order to tame
the scale of the vast reception rooms, such as the observatory
lounge with wraparound windows, a den, and a vast
library, Tino placed comfortable, oversized furniture, and,
working with the owner, hung his impressive collection of
contemporary artwork. Since the client is a voracious reader,
his spacious, well-stocked library, unusual for a yacht,
is a key feature and personal refuge.

"REFLECTING THE INDIVIDUALITY OF OUR CLIENT, *PLANET 9* FEELS STRIKINGLY DIFFERENT TO OTHER BOATS, THROUGH THE SELECTION OF CHARACTERFUL MATERIALS, FURTHERED BY THE USE OF VARIED VINTAGE FURNITURE." ANTOINE DE SIGY

FACING PAGE, TOP
In the observatory lounge with sweeping 180-degree views from the upper deck, Tino designed the wraparound banquette to include mahogany glass-holders and flexible reading lights. An eye-catching group of three different cocktail tables designed by Robsjohn-Gibbings works perfectly with the sofa layout. "Robsjohn-Gibbings's nautically styled furniture seemed like a great fit for the interiors of this yacht, with its practical, restrained, but carefully considered detailing that I very much admire," says Tino.

FACING PAGE, BOTTOM
In the observatory lounge, Robsjohn-Gibbings's slat-backed chairs and Carlo de Carli's black table sit on Tino's carpet. Tino also designed Roman blinds, made of different colors of linen and appliquéd with a pattern inspired by the horizon.

ABOVE
The surprisingly large library includes a meeting table, a desk, and a sitting area; it serves as both a private study and a meeting space, when necessary. The indirect lighting makes the room shimmer, adding intrigue, sophistication, and intimacy.

FACING PAGE
In a guest cabin, an aptly placed artwork of a circular window playfully suggests a porthole with a further view out. The bright yellow felt chair and red vintage telephone pick up colors from the luxurious, multi-stripe carpet woven in Tibet.

ABOVE, LEFT
The corridor's watery carpet design is woven by Bartholomeus in Belgium. The artworks that hang along the corridor showcase a collection of vintage views of early twentieth-century luxury cruise ships.

ABOVE, RIGHT
In the owner's lobby a table by German designer Ingo Maurer has a constellation of nearly invisible LEDs sandwiched between two slices of glass. The fitted cupboards are upholstered in a geometric fabric handwoven in Dakar by Aïssa Dione and detailed with dark wacapou edging.

RIGHT
Looking out toward the deck, the holographic ceiling light is another Ingo Maurer creation.

HOUSING
A COLLECTION

Tino Zervudachi profoundly understands the way in which a superior art collection can enhance an interior. "Paintings or objects absolutely vitalize a room because they express the owner's taste and eye," he says. The aesthetic challenge is to be confident enough to mix things up and create the perfect balance. Tino dares to personalize; he has gleaned a reputation for seamlessly marrying priceless works with pieces of unequal value. "Objects carry a certain kind of magic," he says. "If they represent meaning to the owner, they can stimulate a dialogue and tell a personal story." Most important, there are no rules: white walls can emphasize amazing art, just as a judicious selection of textiles, carpets, and wall colors can superbly enhance the placement of a collection.

FACING PAGE
Tino changed the home's circulation by transforming a former artist's studio and an office into the entrance hall. In front of a breathtaking Francis Bacon, a 1950s brass suspension lamp hangs above Carlo de Carli's table surrounded by nineteenth-century English white-painted dining chairs, standing on a Tino-designed oval carpet, made by Veedon Fleece.

ARTIST'S STUDIO REIMAGINED, LONDON

A renowned British collector acquired a series of artists' studios and houses in Chelsea. Tino Zervudachi's commission was to create a spectacular space for his extraordinary collection, which would be a stylish and comfortable home and also include room for his extended family. "The result is a surprising amount of lateral living space which is unusual for London," offers the client. A complex and lengthy project, it was elaborated over a number of years because the five properties were acquired separately. Working with the architect Chris Mitchell and Sam Bentley from his London office, Tino's principal objective was to forge unity, subtly tying the disparate buildings together. New staircases were built to access different levels between the houses and Tino turned one of the former studios into a big entrance hall, keeping the walls plain in order to enhance the breathtaking range of paintings. "The art looks fantastic but it's casual and the house doesn't feel gallery-like," enthuses the client. Like most impassioned collectors, he knew where to hang his most important pictures, while Tino sensed where bespoke furniture and carpets were required. Outside, Tino transformed two newly acquired exterior spaces into delightful, tiled courtyard patios. "It's one of my favorite homes," says the well-travelled client. "Put it this way, I hate leaving."

FACING PAGE
In the enormously high-ceilinged principal studio room, an astonishing collection of twentieth-century paintings cohabit with a nineteenth-century French iron chandelier and rug inspired by a traditional Tibetan tiger carpet design.

ABOVE, LEFT
Graphic twentieth-century art, and music, share space and strike a dynamic effect.

ABOVE, RIGHT
Tino designed the staircase lined with bookcases for the owner's art books that leads down to the ground-floor studio and dining room.

"THIS HOUSE IS REALLY PERFECT FOR ME. TINO CREATED OPEN,
LATERAL LIVING SPACES, VERY UNUSUAL FOR LONDON.
I CAN'T PUT MY FINGER ON IT, BUT ALTHOUGH THERE ARE SPECTACULAR
WORKS OF ART, HE MAKES IT ALL LOOK VERY NATURAL," SAYS THE CLIENT

Tino entirely reimagined the master bedroom suite by designing a large coved cornice, to help conceal air conditioning and lighting, as well as reconfiguring a muddle of small spaces by opening up rooms to each other through a large double doorway with natural oak detailing. Ikat-bordered curtains in the bathroom frame the Chelsea view.

The neighboring home was purchased in order to connect its garden to the studio. Giving an exotic and unexpected look to the patio, Tino created a courtyard that was tiled with encaustic tiles and a Zellige-covered banquette and fountain.

ALPINE SOPHISTICATION

In a much sought-after mountain resort, an elegant French couple acquired a property with breathtaking views that was to be transformed into the perfect setting for their remarkable collection. Tino Zervudachi's brief was to create a single chalet from a building that had been designed as two apartments. This required reimagining the layouts, to create reception rooms, a spacious master suite, and comfortable new guest rooms, as well as adding service and storage areas. The clients did not want a traditional chalet with rustic wood interiors, but a modern interpretation that was unique and sophisticated. Although Tino was constrained by the existing low ceilings, he succeeded in developing comfortable and elegant interiors that feature the art in the manner of an urban apartment, while embracing the surrounding mountain landscape. The neutral palette is enlivened with splashes of brilliant color from the ikat textiles used throughout the home. As an element of surprise, Tino turned the low ceilings into a design feature with intricate decorative schemes subtly executed by Laurent Chwast. The palette choices inspired by the art, rich fabrics, and textured plastered finishes infuse the spaces with a level of low-key refinement rarely attained in an Alpine setting.

FACING PAGE
A view leading from the dining room into the living room. Tino designed the ceiling with wide, brushed and patinated wood cornices that encircle a hand-painted geometric scheme, to give the illusion of more height. A gray oak table and red upholstered chairs sit on a kilim from Galerie Triff in Paris.

RIGHT
The abstract linear artwork in conversation with the ceiling painting. Enhancing the client's art collection, Tino keeps the walls simple using a black and ecru tweed fabric by Holland & Sherry, finished with a specially made red and black braid. The table is by Christophe Delcourt and the chairs are Cassina.

PAGES 158–59
"The timber detailing on the living room's walls was designed to create panels that offer more verticality to the horizontal walls," says Tino, who chose a background of gray hues for a multi-period collection of art and furniture that includes a pair of tables by André Dubreuil. Exuberant bespoke details are

Nelly Munthe's carpet and silk ikat-bordered curtains. Tino was inspired by the palette of one of the paintings that hangs in the room to create a delicate, Albers-like design on the low ceilings.

ABOVE
In the library, Tino combines the simple elegance of dark tobacco-colored canvas walls in *toile de cocher* by Antoine d'Albiousse, with an eggplant-colored velvet by Nya Nordiska for the deep-cushioned corner sofa. The two French Directoire fauteuils upholstered in a pale green Le Manach Toile de Tours, contrast with McCollin Bryan's hockey-puck-shaped, concrete coffee table.

FACING PAGE
McCollin Bryan's console table, made from scagliola, invigorates the arched hallway.

RIGHT
The small cinema room
was imagined with
two levels and defines
cozy and comfortable
via custom love seats
covered in warm pink
Dominique Kieffer velvet,
and Le Manach-covered
cotton mattress seats
and cushions.

CHELSEA LIGHT, LONDON

"I remember when he came to see an Antony Gormley show and he got so excited," says Thaddaeus Ropac. For twenty years, Tino lived happily in a raised ground-floor Belgravia apartment with soaring ceilings. A need for more space, however, led to his hunt for a larger London apartment—a lateral conversion—that felt more open, with a view on the surrounding trees. This one encompasses the second floor of three townhouses and boasts windows at both the front and the back—benefiting from east and west light as well as superb views—and still remains within a stone's throw of his office. The apartment had gracious spaces, with 12 foot high ceilings, including elegant bow windows, reception rooms at the back, and spacious bedrooms at the front. Little architectural work was required, as it had been carefully developed previously, and Tino only had to decorate. This marked a first. For this easy and enjoyable process, he purchased new pieces and brought in furniture and objects from other homes, mixing different styles and periods, and even kept the grisaille landscape wallpaper from the original dining room. Certain obstacles were encountered, not least the installation by crane of Tino's 880-pound (400-kilo) Antony Gormley sculpture, while the Robert Longo drawing of trees had to be hoisted up by specially constructed scaffolding through the window, which itself had to be removed. Instead of choosing curtains for the salon, Tino designed blinds interplaying with the room's architecture, which enhance the large bow window. Comfortable, filled with light and some of his favorite belongings, this Chelsea apartment feels like home.

LEFT
A pair of Louis XV gilded chairs, in dark green silk-velvet, flank the door whose lines-and-circles motif is echoed throughout the apartment, giving character to the doors.

FACING PAGE
The guest bedroom has a muffled, padded comfort thanks to the walls in green Alcantara and a carpet of smooth baize. The eighteenth-century Neapolitan bed from Louis Bofferding has cushions made out of Robert Kime's Harlequin hand-dyed silk ikat. The dark scheme was chosen to show the eclectic collection of twentieth- and twenty-first-century works on paper. The unusually deep nineteenth-century English armchair is upholstered in Le Manach's Vache fabric.

RIGHT
Lines of paint frame
the walls and windows to
emphasize the drawing
room's architectural shape,
while Antony Gormley's
cast-iron sculpture
stands soldier-like by the
window. Tino designed
the striped carpet
to give a sense of width
to the room. In the bow
window, the metal
base of the oval table,
designed by André
Dubreuil, gives lightness
and allows the surface
to float. In the foreground
stands a Henry Moore
sculpture on a marble-
topped table by Adnet.

LEFT
The mirror above
the nineteenth-century
marble fireplace reflects
Robert Longo's charcoal
drawing, a mobile
by Jean Collet,
and a third-century
terra-cotta ceremonial
drinking vessel.

FACING PAGE
An unusually large
Louis XVI provincial
chaise longue is
a favorite place to work
by the bow window.
Beside it is a gilded
Louis XIV marble-topped
table on which stands
an Indonesian wooden
figure and 1960s Italian
Cobra lamp.

FACING PAGE
In the guest bathroom, delicately backlit glass shelves display eighteenth-century famille verte vases and a Jean Cocteau bronze sculpture of a double-faced profile.

BELOW, LEFT
A set of William Wegman photographs of Labradors are hung on the dressing room doors.

BELOW, RIGHT
The master bedroom with caramel-colored Alcantara walls and blue bound cream curtains. The half tester bed adds warmth to the high-ceilinged room.

COMPOSED COMFORT, LONDON

A European collector looking for a London pied-à-terre found this terraced townhouse in the perfect location. Moving from Paris, the client was aiming to create a lighthearted and joyful home that was devoid of pretension. Though the house was in relatively good condition, the spatial arrangement was awkward, and it was necessary to reconfigure the whole of the interior. Tino Zervudachi enlarged the drawing room, added an elevator, and redesigned the bedrooms, dressing rooms, and bathrooms, as well as installing a coffered ceiling to achieve the paneling in the wide entrance hall, unusually large for a small London house, that leads into the bright and spacious square living room. He commissioned new pieces to harmonize with the owner's collection of paintings

and furniture from other houses, including a jewel-toned lacquered table with inset pieces of onyx by Mattia Bonetti, and a stylish bronze coffee table by Valentin Loellmann. Tino relied on monochromatic colors and designed a hand-painted canvas wallpaper with shadowed stripes for the living room walls to give verticality to the low-ceilinged space. The room boasts three framed windows with a view to a whole series of neighboring gardens, creating the impression of being in the country. The lower-ground-floor kitchen opens onto a fresh and informal patio garden furnished with a geranium-red dining table and chairs. Tino dynamized the space with light and greenery by adding mirroring behind the trelliswork, succeeding in opening up the viewless space and giving it depth.

LEFT
A corner of the living room is livened up by an orange lacquered side table, inset with pieces of onyx, created by the French designer Mattia Bonetti, on which stand favorite objects and sculpture.

FACING PAGE
In the entrance hall, André Dubreuil's gueridon and a pair of vintage Chiavari Tre Archi chairs stand on a circular rug designed by Tino, inspired by Sonia Delaunay. It is similar to the one Tino commissioned for his rue des Beaux-Arts apartment in Paris in 1999.

RIGHT
RIGHT
The Freshwest Stupa
table from Rosie Uniacke
sits on Nelly Munthe's
specially commissioned
dhurrie.

"I THINK TINO SURPRISED ME BECAUSE EVEN THOUGH I THOUGHT I KNEW
WHAT I WANTED TO DO, HE HAD FURTHER SUGGESTIONS. IT WAS NICE HAVING
THE ENTHUSIASM FOR MY IDEAS FROM SOMEONE I REALLY RESPECTED." TATIANA CASIRAGHI

PAGES 176–77
In the square living room,
Nelly Munthe's rug
adds unity to the whole
scheme, including the
blue sofa and Louis XVI
bergère chairs
upholstered in Robert
Kime's Harlequin silk ikat.

ABOVE
The elegant lower-
ground kitchen and
family room are lit by
a trellised patio with
a mirrored back to
create space and light,
enhanced by the pop
of color from Fermod's
Poppy Red outdoor
furniture.

FACING PAGE
A close-up of the
paneling and details
of the wrought-iron
balustrade design, which
Tino simplified to suggest
a ribbon-like movement.
Manuela Zervudachi's
graceful alabaster
and bronze wall light
illuminates the way up
the stairs—carpeted
in a stylish, dark silk and
cotton runner, with red
and cream striped
border, by Vanderhurd.

LEFT BANK CALM, PARIS

When a new client decided to transform her home, she hired the architect Annabelle Seldorf "to bring in light and change the volumes." When this work was completed, she then called upon Tino's expertise for the decoration and furnishing of the rooms. "I knew what I wanted but wasn't sure how to get it," she says. For twenty-five years, the client had lived in the apartment in a completely different way. Its previous 1980s décor by François Catroux was brimming with lots of pattern and objects. However, she wanted a real departure—a clean, contemplative, and restful interior. The spaces that Selldorf designed seamlessly express the client's needs. Tino's role, however, was to bring the architectural shell to life without losing sight of its simplicity. After their first meeting, the client felt reassured. "Tino understood everything," she says. The designer adopted a palette of natural materials in monochromatic shades, helped source furniture, and suggested artwork, focusing on a pared-down selection of beautiful pieces. "Tino has this flair for walking into a place and finding three things immediately," the client says. Case in point: an eccentric 1940s Italian mirror found in a Left Bank antique shop. "It's perfect, but was presented by Tino in such a humble fashion," she recalls. The only disagreement concerned the seating area giving onto the intimate garden designed by Louis Benech. "Tino was worried that the two sofas— placed opposite each other— would seem like the seating in a train carriage, but then he agreed that it worked," she says. To accentuate the salon's dimensions and tie in the client's handsome collection which includes fine Augsburg silver objects, an Anselm Kiefer was acquired as well as other twentieth- and twenty-first century pieces. Tino designed three abstract carpets, woven by Galerie Diurne. "They are extraordinary," says the client. "Patterned rugs would have been too busy. His carpets strike the right echo between all the belongings." When mutual trust drives the design process, the result is harmonious.

LEFT
Looking towards the living room, in the foreground a bronze sculpture by Claude Lalanne, and beyond an asymmetrical 1940s Italian beveled mirror add a quirky touch to the elegant room, along with Ron Arad's rocking chair.

FACING PAGE
In the dining room, Tino teamed the Gio Ponti chairs, upholstered in Le Crin's horse hair, with his own designed tables, made by Christian Mussy, and an angular ceiling light by Apparatus. A pair of photos by Antoine Schneck flank Ignazio Gardella's 1950s bookcases.

PAGES 182–83
Calm reigns in the large ground-floor space looking onto the Louis Benech-designed garden. Tranquility is further extended by the choice of Finn Juhl's sofas, Ado Chale's coffee table, and the composition of Gio Ponti chairs. "Thanks to Annabelle Selldorf's marvelous bay window, it's a wonderful place for the client to read and to contemplate," says Tino.

BELOW
"The pair of eighteenth-century portraits are unlikely candidates for the contemporary interior, but they work because they are part of the client's story," notes Tino. Meanwhile, the rugs Tino designed unite the client's collection and the surrounding rooms.

FACING PAGE
The smaller living room's atmosphere and elegance are enhanced by Tino's carpet and a restrained color-palette using Sylvie Johnson fabrics, specially woven, for the cushions. Both the lamp and bronze cube are by Philippe Anthonioz. Marc du Plantier's painting, which allows a continuation of the garden into the house, was found at the Biennale des Antiquaires—"I didn't hesitate," remembers the client.

FACING PAGE
In the living room, Manuela Zervudachi's ceramic *Space Cloud* sculpture is teamed with Mauro Fabbro's lamp, sourced at Alexandre Biaggi's gallery, while the Tino four-seater sofa is upholstered in Dedar's celadon-colored velvet.

ABOVE
A painting by Anselm Kiefer sets the tone in the ground-floor living room. "The painting between the windows had to be spectacular," says Tino. "Very 'gut-instinct,' but I knew it would work," agrees the client. Elegant curtains bound with tiny black edges stand either side of the artwork. The multi-footed walnut coffee table is by Tom Tramel, created in 1968, and the pair of armchairs are by Gustavo Pulitzer-Finali and covered in a Sylvie Johnson custom-woven fabric.

LEFT
The simple but refined leather-upholstered balustrade that Tino imagined in order to elevate its finish.

EMBRACING THE SUN

Having spent the summers of his childhood and adult life in the Mediterranean, the sun is part of Tino Zervudachi's DNA. "Many places I deal with are not for those shy of heat, but I love a hot climate," he admits. Understanding the Mediterranean lifestyle, Tino Zervudachi designs houses that work and are practical; for example, he avoids using silk—"It rots in the sun," he says—and knows where to create terraces with nearby cushion storage for when sudden storms hit. "Often, I'm creating an environment or fantasy world for people in holiday mode," he explains. "An escape that has nothing to do with their lives outside of that." Ever mindful of how natural light can determine a way of living and decorating interiors and exteriors, Tino offers that certain rules need to be observed. "It is essential to allow for shaded spaces for hot summers as well as sun-filled spaces, for mid-season," he says. Nor can the evening be forgotten. "At night, one wants to be dining under the stars," he says.

FACING PAGE
Up on the teak deck of Tino's motor yacht *Mabrouka*, the canvas awning offers shade while the lunch table doubles as a big central daybed. "In Arabic, *mabrouka* means lucky," says Tino.

PAGES 190–91
The yacht was built in Gosport, in 1926, by Camper & Nicholson, who were considered the best shipbuilders in the world at that time. *Mabrouka* seamlessly fits in with Hydra's carless lifestyle, where groceries are delivered by mule.

MABROUKA

Tino Zervudachi and his partner Louis-Charles de Remusat always wanted a boat. Through a family friend, they found a vintage motor yacht for sale in Cannes built by the historical shipbuilder Camper & Nicholson. It would complement their lifestyle in Hydra, by allowing daily swimming excursions to protected bays and lunches on board, as well as the occasional cruise. Built in 1926, the golden era of the shipyard, *Mabrouka* was originally designed to cruise the Solent, between England's mainland and the Isle of Wight. Tino reimagined the vessel for the Mediterranean, rethinking the upholstery and the layout of the interior spaces. He recovered the dark-red leather cushions with white linen, padded and contrast-overstitched to create stripes. Tino also restored and repolished all the original paneling, adding light fixtures and rugs, as well as hanging works by contemporary photographers such as Aramy Machry and Tim Hall. Up on the main deck, Tino turned a former table and two benches into a big central daybed that doubles as a lunch table. When first acquiring *Mabrouka* in 2014, Tino did a minor refit, but six years later he replaced the engines, and put in a generator and air conditioning. Though modernized, *Mabrouka* retains its magical old-world romance and glamour, one that matches beautifully with the understated lifestyle of Hydra.

FACING PAGE
Tino retained, restored and repolished *Mabrouka*'s original 1926 wood paneling— a combination of mahogany and walnut. He also created the secret door that leads from one cabin to a bathroom.

ABOVE, LEFT
The banquette seating is recovered in a white linen fabric, that Tino Zervudachi had padded and overstitched in contrasting vertical stripes.

ABOVE, RIGHT
In the guest cabin, Rifat Ozbek's Yastik cushion adds color and an exotic touch, while an historic, signed photograph of *Mabrouka*, by Beken of Cowes, the famous maritime photographer of the 1920s, hangs above.

RIGHT
A detail of the staircase and the corridor that leads to the galley, where a circular mirror hangs above the doorway to create a sense of depth and height.

ESCAPE TO GREECE, HYDRA

Ever since Tino can remember, he always wanted to own a home in Greece. When working on another project in Hydra, his dream came true. The house he found was in terrible condition, far from the Greek idyll he had imagined, as everything—the floors, ceilings, woodwork, and walls—was dark brown! The interior of the house resembled a gloomy bunker, though there was a finely tiled and sturdy roof that was in excellent shape, and Tino realized that the house was peaceful, and the location was perfect, with an exceptionally beautiful view across the village. His goal was to transform the property into a typical Greek island home. It was a major undertaking: the interiors were stripped and entirely reconfigured, the walls were replastered, and the ceilings repainted or remade, while the floors and windows were replaced. Since there are no cars on Hydra all the construction materials had to be lugged up from the port by donkey. Working with architect Dimitri Papacharalampous and contractor Petros Kritikos, Tino converted the ground-floor storeroom into a kitchen, added guest rooms, poured polished-concrete floors, and redesigned the new staircase that opened out into the light-filled living room. A combination of new furniture and belongings from past homes fills the space with fond memories. For the summer months lived outside, Tino created four decks to catch the light and views, while cozy sitting areas are shaded by bamboo pergolas on either side of a swimming pool edged with cypresses. Nearby, a short allée of citrus trees produce baskets of lemons. Tino Zervudachi's Hydra is the perfect place to recuperate and hide away from a frantically paced working life.

LEFT
In the living room, Tino redesigned the staircase leading to the main bedroom. Objects from his travels over the years populate the space, including a bamboo amphora from Africa, a stone carving from Indonesia, and a glowing work by Howard Hodgkin.

FACING PAGE
The hallway is embellished with an eclectic mix of objects such as the wave sculpture by Maggi Hambling and leather folding chair by Mogen Koch, from the 1960s.

A Jean-Michel Frank
sofa bed invites to relax.
"I wanted the peace of
this island to be reflected
in how the house feels
to me," Tino says.
The all-white walls
and ceilings with gray
woodwork evoke a
traditional Greek style,
and over all there
is an "undesigned" feel,
created by the informal
collection of different
objects, such as
the unusual "Giraffe"
standing lamp by
François Thévenin.

"AT THE START OF EACH PROJECT, TINO DASHES OFF A SERIES OF QUICK SKETCHES THAT ARE AN INTEGRAL PART OF HIS CREATIVE PROCESS. AMAZINGLY, THE END RESULT IS ALMOST IDENTICAL TO HIS FIRST NOTES AND SHOW THAT HE ALREADY HAD EVERYTHING IN HIS HEAD FROM THE VERY BEGINNING." PHILIPPE ANTHONIOZ

BELOW
In the bedroom, a Bhutanese fabric covers the foot of the bed while the windows are simply curtained with C & C Milano twill. The fish-shaped chaise longue in cane was designed by Lina Zervudaki.

FACING PAGE
The passageway becomes architecturally interesting by the use of timber arches, and ironwork-covered fan lights that bring light into the adjacent spaces.

RIGHT
Inspired by the
exceptional view
of Hydra—particularly
at sunset—Tino created
an all-encompassing
outside terrace. An ideal
place for entertainment,
friends and family gather
on the wraparound
built-in seat, in front
of which stand a specially
designed pair of low
tables crafted by
Tom Powell.

RIVIERA MODERN, PROVENCE

The Côte d'Azur conceals many astonishing properties, but this lavish estate—one of the largest in the area—boasts many acres of olive and pine trees, two swimming pools, and two tennis courts, as well as an official heliport. It was acquired as a vacation home for friends and family by a longstanding client, and Tino understood that the 1970s concrete compound needed a serious upgrade. The building was composed of a series of boxy, uninteresting spaces, resembling an airport lounge, with multiple reception areas. He needed to bring logic to the maze of rooms that had been built with little regard for style. Tino began the re-design by re-configuring all the interior spaces, to create logical relationships between rooms, needing to reposition some windows to bring in more light. A new terrace was created, connecting two wings of the house. To generate visual interest and to unify the spaces architecturally, Tino imposed bold, fluted plasterwork walls for the living room, entrance hall and staircase leading down into the dining room, creating a metrical language. Finally, he re-colored the houses exterior to blend in with the rocky landscape behind. Tino also assembled an impressive collection of furniture that he commissioned or designed and sourced vintage pieces such as armchairs by Jean-Charles Moreux, a console table by Robsjohn-Gibbings, and an armoire by André Sornay. The bespoke garden and terrace furniture was especially designed by Tino and made by Tectona. In response to the client's request for a home cinema, Tino transformed the former gym, and designed the luxurious chaises longues, which he teamed with tables by Jean-Marc Lelouch. To emphasize the relaxed but modern style, furnishings were kept simple—mostly linens and cottons in muted colors—allowing the amazing views of the Bay to take center stage.

RIGHT
"When we created that window with a view towards the sea, it felt like it needed an exceptional piece of sculpture, to be placed in front," Tino says. Manuela Zervudachi's dramatic *Space Flower* sculpture commands the roof terrace, while Noé Duchaufour-Lawrance's sculpture light hangs from the ceiling, casting concentric circles of light onto the stairs below.

LEFT
The enfilade from the library to the living room, where the furniture combination focuses on a steel gueridon by Georges Geffroy, circa 1960, the legendary designer at Jansen and a stylish pair of Mahogany bergères by J-C Moreux.

FACING PAGE
In the entrance hall, a Philippe Anthonioz bronze lantern is suspended above two Tino designs—a metal and lacquer topped table made by Christian Mussy and Ateliers Gohard, and an oval flat-weave rug commissioned from Shyam Ahuja. The doors leading into the living room are covered in marbleized paper by Tanguy Flameng, using the Japanese suminagashi technique.

RIGHT
Framing the bold and breathtaking view of the villa's garden set against the backdrop of the Mediterranean, Tino designed a pair of bronze-framed coffee tables with layered plaster panels—inspired by Ben Nicholson plaster-relief works—topped with glass, which rest between the two large sofas. The striped plaster-relief walls add a vibrancy to the boxy room as do Tino's undulating embroidered curtain-borders, made by Maximiliano Modesti.

The four-poster bed was designed to harmonize with the Robsjohn-Gibbings daybed, which rests by the Paul McCobb armchair. The flat-woven carpet designed by Tino and made by Shyam Ahuja lends a playful character to the room, while a pair of blue painted stools, sourced by Antoine de Sigy, add a sense of light and airy holiday zest.

Arabescato marble lines the walls of the master bathroom, creating a luxurious atmosphere. A leather-topped bronze stool by Philippe Anthonioz stands by the bathtub, with spectacular views to the sea. "Philippe's work is contemporary, but it feels like antiquity at the same time," says Tino. "The incredible strength of his creations complements the straight lines of this house's slightly brutalist architecture."

BELOW, LEFT
In the awkwardly proportioned dining room, different layers of decoration include Tino's ceiling treatment (painted by Laurent Chwast), a vast table commissioned from Kostia, and Tino's embroidered cushions, inspired by Matisse's cut-outs and made by Maximiliano Modesti.

BELOW, RIGHT
A never-ending swimming pool looks onto the bay. The terrace has B & B Italia chaises longues, teak side-tables, and Tucci sun umbrellas.

FACING PAGE
The home cinema lies behind a terrace of planted olive trees. Tino imagined the media room, a former gym, with comfortable oak-framed chaises longues, which he designed with sleigh-like features. The dark, cherry-wood paneled room with built-in bookcases also doubles up as a reading room. A summery air is achieved by simple bound-edged linen curtains.

"TINO IS LIKE A CREATIVE PRINCE BECAUSE HE IS TRUSTWORTHY AND POSSESSES SUCH SERENITY, GRACE, AND INTELLIGENCE WITHIN HIS WORK." PHILIPPE ANTHONIOZ

FINCA HAVEN, IBIZA

This once dilapidated finca situated on a large tract of fertile land in the north of Ibiza needed revitalizing. The property retained some of its original features, like an ancient olive press—"there are still footprints from where a donkey went round and round," says the owner—and had until recently belonged to a German woman who was known for her weekly hippie markets, which she hosted on the grounds; the markets were well attended during the 1960s and 1970s. However, when Tino's client bought the property, everything was in terrible condition. For years, no maintenance work had been done, until the roof began to fall in. Tino gutted and redesigned everything, including the layout of the gardens, lily pond, and swimming pool. He worked with Juan Macedo, choosing plants and designing the different garden areas: "It now has great fruit trees—apricot, grapefruit, and pomegranate," says the client, who had had no preconceptions about what the house could become. "I wanted to enlarge the three bedrooms," he recalls, "but Tino insisted that we keep them the existing, original sizes, so as to maintain the integrity of the architecture, because my family and friends would be living outdoors. He was right." It was important to Tino to maintain the authentic quality of the finca, but carefully bringing in light into the previously dark rooms creating a relaxed atmosphere. The woodwork, plasterwork, and flooring were entirely rethought and redesigned and everything made by local craftsmen. He kept it very spontaneous and spare, allowing textiles to bring warmth and charm. "It resonates because of his great use of colors and natural ability to choose," enthuses the client. "Tino is very clever at putting the bohemian and the artisanal together."

PAGES 214–15
To further the finca's charm and authenticity, Tino only worked with local artisans, entirely rethinking the layout of the old farmhouse, creating skylights for direct sunshine, micro-cement floors, and designing black steel-framed doors onto the loggia and terraces. A small pair of antique doors—found in an antiques store in Ibiza—access the storage space under the stairs. The striped hemp rug is from Shyam Ahuja.

BELOW
Tino converted an agricultural shed with corrugated-plastic roof into this light-bathed, beamed breakfast room that opens onto the garden and landscape beyond, leading to the ancient olive press and toward the newly created inner courtyard. "We put in 'sabine' beams and created a wide, arched steel window, facing the view," he says. The chairs are by Bonacina and the 1960s oak table sourced in Paris.

FACING PAGE
In the narrow TV room made from two small rooms with very high ceilings, Tino designed a buttoned daybed, and simple de Le Cuona linen curtains. A Spanish Moorish-inspired textile covers the armchairs. The kilim-covered ottoman, Moroccan lanterns, inlaid table, and cushions made from antique Suzani textiles evoke an exotic touch and draw attention to one of the client's favorite paintings.

TOP LEFT
Tino designed the pergola in the courtyard and, with Juan Macedo, planted it with saffron and white bougainvillea. The space is paved with flagstones of local stone and features an ample, sprawling banquette, spread with cushions colored like the blooming plants. By the gate, leading to the orchard, there are bamboo chairs from Liggestolen. "It is a special place to have drinks and eat in the evening, looking across the valley at the agricultural land beyond," Tino says.

BOTTOM LEFT
Tino designed the swimming pool in a former vineyard. "We moved the vines down to the lower level," he says. The pool is painted a darkish gray, allowing the water to turn green and blend in with the vegetation.

RIGHT
In a guest bathroom/
dressing room, Tino
designed cupboard and
bathroom doors, based
on an old shutter found
in the barn. A shower is
concealed behind the
double doors. The newly
wood-paneled ceiling
lends the space warmth
and depth.

LEFT
The living room's coral
stone columns belonged
to the former house and
remain the only feature
kept by Tino in the new
design. Unusually located
in the center of the
space, the long, gilded
chaise is reupholstered
in a Jennifer Shorto fabric.
"It is where everyone
either comes in and lies
down or throws their
stuff," says the client.

NASSAU BEACH HOUSE, BAHAMAS

Seeking out warmth in the winter, a couple whom Tino
Zervudachi had worked with on many European projects,
including their yacht, went house-hunting in Nassau.
"We had no interest in buying a plot and building something
new," the client says. They found a house which had been
on the market for some time. "It was on a street we loved—
location, location, location—it had its own beach and
the right number of bedrooms," she explains. However,
everything was painted dark brown, the wooden furniture
was clunky, and the interiors gloomy, with a desperately
overgrown garden. "But the bones of the house were
fabulous. And it was built with solid walls—not always the
case here." Since she and her husband trusted Tino, they
patiently waited for him to become available. After a day
of studying the house, he understood how to achieve its
bright and cheerful potential. Working with Kiko Sanchez's
team of architects, Tino envisioned a grand beach house,
rearranging the spaces completely, transforming the pool
area, and reworking the ceiling designs. In the newly created
room that now houses the kitchen, for instance, the ceiling
was lowered, to create better proportions. "Tino absolutely
revolutionized the spaces, transforming the inside," recalls
the client. "People who knew the house before didn't even
recognize it once we moved in." Furniture was both bought,
and sourced from the client's collection: "Tino was horrified
to be asked to use grand English and French furniture at
the beach but I said, 'We must use what we have in storage,
because it's a waste not to,'" she says. So, unlikely pieces
were entirely reimagined to work in the new spaces and
to create an elegant feel, while still working in the Caribbean
setting. "It gives the place character," notes the client.
Meanwhile, her light gray bedroom is "absolutely divine and
dreamy. Tino gets comfort and he gets living," she says.

Tino found the unusual
hat stand in Paris. "He
rang and said, 'I think
I've seen the right one,'"
recalls the client. "Made
to look like coral, it's
perfection—the needed
splash of color," she says.

"In the living room, we
liked the idea of mixing in
some quite grand pieces
of furniture—like a gilded
eighteenth-century
English side table and
mirror—with a pair of
more beach-like cane
chairs," says Tino.
"Regency chairs are
covered in linens rather
than brocade." The goal
was to evoke a grand
beach feel. The Crosshatch
ceiling light is from
Ironies in New York.

ABOVE

In the master bedroom, a Queen Anne chair is covered in Jennifer Shorto linen. Tino found the antique Chinese fisherman's smock made of bamboo, in New York. The desk is Karl Springer from Lobel Modern and the lamp is from Robert Kuo, with flooring made from the local coquina stone.

FACING PAGE

The enchanting four-poster bed was designed by Tino and made in New York: "I was inspired by a photo of Bunny Mellon's bedroom in Antigua," he says. The gray-striped linen on the headboard is from Nobilis and the rug is custom Holland & Sherry.

FACING PAGE
Tino raised and entirely redesigned the pool area. "It was previously very awkward and three feet lower," he says. To the right, a bridge connects the terrace to the beach. Referred to as Lucy's Bridge by the client's family, it is named after Lucy Singh, who worked with Tino on the project. "You sit on the terrace and just stare at the water, which changes all the time," says the client. "We placed the upside-down sculpture—*Les Pieds au Mur* by French sculptor Philippe Berry—at the horizon line to create an element of surprise and fun," says Tino.

ABOVE
The covered terrace is furnished with pieces from Walters Wicker, upholstered in their white fabric, and cushions in Kuba fabric from St. Frank. The Indonesian wooden carving, sourced by Tino in New York, adds to the exotic atmosphere.

"IT'S TRUE THAT TINO HAS AN EXCEPTIONAL AND OUTSTANDING TALENT, BUT HE'S ALSO TOTALLY PASSIONATE ABOUT HIS PROFESSION,"

SAYS THE CLIENT

COLLECTOR'S HIDEAWAY, GREECE

The renowned gallery owner Thaddaeus Ropac wanted a summer house in Greece. He knew Patmos, Porto Heli, and Spetses, but was particularly struck by Hydra. "It feels like the most bohemian and laidback of the islands," he says. "That sense of 1960s history linked to Leonard Cohen and all his artist friends remains." Tino Zervudachi found a house for Thaddeus through an old friend. "He showed me pictures and I fell in love," recalls Thaddeus. "My idea was to keep it as simple as possible." Pierre Pelegry was very involved, choosing furniture from the Galerie Eric Philippe. Tino chose to work with architect Dimitri Papacharalampous and Louis Benech was brought in to design the garden and the terraces. Formerly separated into apartments, the house was badly divided and needed a complete rearrangement. "There was a blocked-up entrance on an upper street-level and Tino suggested opening it up," Ropac explains.

This involved moving the kitchen from the lower- to the upper-street level adjacent to the newly created dining terrace, allowing deliveries—by mule—right to the door and creating more bedrooms downstairs. Wall space was added by eliminating doorways. "That was important for larger works such as Alex Katz's *Seagull*, a painting always destined for my house by the sea," Ropac says. Tino's sunny nature and endless innovations never stopped impressing him. "He made a little guest room out of a gardener's shed," Ropac says. "It meant drilling deep into the rock." Tino also transformed the roof into a terrace, which is now a principal entertaining space, which had never even been used before. "Tino redid everything," enthuses Ropac. "He also knew exactly where to put our pool. It is too small to swim in, but it is wonderful to sit there and have a glass of wine at sunset."

LEFT
In the living room, two oak, leather, and linen chaises longues, designed in 1963 by Danish designers Preben Fabricius and Jørgen Kastholm, are grouped with Tony Cragg's pots, and a Hans Wegner oak cabinet. "Pierre Pelegry and I had definite ideas of how the house should look," says Thaddaeus Ropac.

FACING PAGE
Outside on the terrace, the ancient jasmine climber grows up the three-story house and is retrained onto the pergola adjacent to the newly built terrace.

PAGES 230–31
The house's poetic
simplicity is enhanced
by the choice of a Jason
Martin white painting,
a 1940s Otto Færge table,
a 1950s Harvey Probber
mahogany table,
a Terrazzo Boomerang
Coffee Table, and a 1950s
floor lamp by Paavo
Tynell. New windows
needed to be made
in the traditional style,
and Tino decided
to open up the room,
originally divided into
two. "I wanted to expose
the beautiful and original
archway," he says.
Meanwhile, the floors,
completed in traditional
Greek flagstones, add
warmth and depth.

BELOW
Stephan Balkenhol's
statue highlights Tino's
painted beam work.

RIGHT
An Anselm Kiefer hangs
above the sofa while
a Georg Baselitz circular
work dominates the
other wall. "Tino got rid
of several doors in order
to add wall space," says
Ropac. The two walnut
side tables are by
Robsjohn-Gibbings,
with a Gordon Martz
lamp on the right-hand
side table.

LEFT
Initially, this space was
a roofless ruin with
a blocked-up doorway
to the upper street.
"We put the roof back on,
creating a room that is
now the kitchen and
made it accessible from
the street," says Tino.
An antique marble
sink and the trellised
cupboards, with access
to a tiny patio for growing
herbs, creates a perfect
Mediterranean kitchen.

TOP RIGHT
Tino transformed
the former toolshed into
an elegant monastic
guestroom. As it is built
into the rock, there are
two levels. Steps are
needed to climb up
to the built-in bed. The
ceramic bedside lamps
are by Marshall Studios.

BOTTOM RIGHT
The pool area where
wine is enjoyed at sunset.
"There wasn't enough
space to have a lap
pool," says Tino, "so,
the idea was to turn
a cooling fountain
into a dipping pool."
Fountain by Not Vital.

RETREATS

Having spent many winter holidays in Switzerland, Tino Zervudachi understands mountain living, and is especially artful when it comes to designing a great chalet. "Life is disciplined by nature and the seasons," he says. As well as the obvious pursuits of skiing in the winter and hiking in the summer, the emphasis on indoor/outdoor living is primordial, and he understands that creating a home for mountain living calls for designs dictated by combining spectacular views and a cozy atmosphere, while also being familiar with contemporary architecture driven by the lifestyle and climate. "Not everyone wants a rustic-styled interior of a traditional chalet," the designer reasons. Working in various styles to suit the personality of different clients is important. "There are often constraints, such as the fixed height of low ceilings, which present challenges of their own," but Tino takes these as a starting point and pushes the boundaries, joining magnificent landscapes with comfortable, contemporary luxury.

FACING PAGE
In the bleak midwinter, a Tino-designed chalet casts a spell.

MOUNTAIN GUEST CHALET

At the top of a steep mountain road where Tino had
already transformed a chalet for a client, the opportunity
arose to acquire the neighboring house to make a guest
chalet. "Tino is so good at figuring out space," says the
client. "And that alone is worth everything." Since the newly
purchased old chalet was small and in poor condition,
Tino and the local architect, Bruno Jori, came up with a
scheme to knock it down, rebuild a new one, and connect
the two buildings with an underground tunnel that cleverly
opens through a bookcase in the old house. "You slide a
bookcase to the right to gain access to an underground
passage that feels like a gallery space and leads to the
newly built four-bedroom chalet with a top-floor living
room for entertaining," enthuses the client. Tino's brief
was to design an easygoing home for the client's children
and grandchildren, as well as showcase his art. He chose
light-colored pine wood for the floors and walls of the
spectacular, double-height living room, with breathtaking,
transversal views across the mountains and the valley.
Tino kept it casual for the client, who is a consummate
host. Aiming for more of a bohemian country house
atmosphere than a typical chalet, he chose rich,
autumnal-hued fabrics, with an eclectic choice of furniture
and fabrics that include oriental embroidery—very
appropriate for a client who began his retail empire
with a block-printing business in Rajasthan.

LEFT
In this spectacular
double-height room,
Tino's considered
accumulation of eclectic
furniture and different
styles created the
impression that this
brand-new building
had evolved over time.
Elegant comfort
emanates from his
fireplace. "During big
parties, people can sit
around it," the client says.
"Above this area, there is
a TV-watching gallery."

LEFT
The staircase is carpeted
in a red dhurrie with
blue bindings and the
Tino-designed handrail
is made of simple
wrought-iron.

FACING PAGE
A bedroom, walled
in a fabric inspired by
Moghul-style trees
and shrubs, references
the client's connection
to India, and is a warm
background to the
nineteenth-century
alpine walnut chest
of drawers.

In the underground playroom and cinema, Tino painted the ceiling green and created an inviting, primary color scheme enhanced by the curtains, made of Kravet's summer-green and blue wool fabric, and a deep green wool felt carpet.

To create a dynamic walk between the two chalets, Tino designed the carpet in the underground corridor in this herringbone-motif, created by Shyam Ahuja. The space was designed to showcase the client's extensive contemporary art collection.

TYROLEAN FISHING LODGE, AUSTRIA

When a family for whom Tino had designed many properties over the years acquired a prime plot of land high up in the Alps, they naturally called upon him to help them achieve their dream fishing lodge. The broad, three-tiered house, lying at the end of an unpaved road, is used mostly as a summer home for fishing. The surrounding forest bristles with red deer, foxes, and wild boar. In spirit, the project was driven by the clients' knowledge of the area—they had rented a nearby property for some decades. The Austrian architect Peter Helletzgruber was called in to design the building and Tino worked with the clients who had in-depth knowledge of the area, to develop the interior decoration of the house. After creating a clearing in the forest, they situated the house at the top of the piece of land, which falls forward onto a rushing Alpine river. Keeping within the local vernacular, the whole interior is fashioned from wood. Relying on the masterful carpentry skills of Anton Gögl, pine paneling lines the walls, while carved beams support the ceilings. To determine the traditional Austrian aesthetic of the home, Tino worked with the clients' collections of painted eighteenth- and nineteenth-century Tyrolean furniture, antique kilims, and art, including incorporating some antique tiled stoves— *kachelöfen*—which were placed throughout the house, and which became sculptural design objects in themselves. Newly made sofas and armchairs are deep and comfortable, and the dining area is made festive by one of the stoves and authentic *Bauernstuhl* chairs and other furniture typical of the region. The result is a romantic and remote fairy-tale home for a contemporary Alpine lifestyle, whose apparent simplicity in style belies tremendous comfort.

RIGHT
Set against a dramatic, craggy mountain, this house was designed by Peter Helletzgruber, styled on a traditional lodge with a steeply pitched roof, dormer windows, and a veranda.

This charming and unusual antique copper front door, when teamed with an early nineteenth-century Austrian tiled stove and mounted by a pair of deer antlers, creates an atmospheric arrival to the lodge.

BELOW
Tino enhanced rural simplicity by combining the client's collection of furniture with new acquisitions. The antique French, green-painted wing chair is upholstered in tan leather and the armchair to the left is covered in Nuages Chinois, a custom-colored jacquard by Prelle.

FACING PAGE
The kitchen's modern appliances are hidden behind rustic cabinetry that dialogues perfectly with the exposed beams. "In this kitchen everything evolved around the client wanting an old wood-burning oven and cooktop," he says.

PAGE 252
A congenial atmosphere was created by mixing elements of the client's collection, such as the traditional green-tiled wood-burning stove known as a *kachelöfen*, antique kilims, and hand-painted parchment lampshades.

PAGE 253
A pair of eighteenth-century beds painted in the local Bauernmalerei folk-art style further the guestroom's charm. "The house's design philosophy was that it had been created slowly over time, through generations," says Tino.

WINTER TRANQUILITY

In an incredible location halfway up a mountain, with outstanding panoramic views, this minimalist chalet has been transformed for a young couple and their children. "It was a real leap in the dark," admits the husband. "But we let Tino's imagination run wild because he's got such amazing taste and he's a family friend." Calm was the key word during the brief, combined with the idea of a sleek, über-contemporary James Bond villain's lair. In spite of the superb location, and the principal room's surprisingly large windows, the house was depressing when the owners acquired it. It had not been touched since the 1970s and retained its orange stained-wood walls with overly carved alpine detailing and different floor finishes in every room, requiring a total overhaul. Working with local contractors, Tino redesigned the staircase balustrade, moved the master bedroom downstairs, took out an obstructing partition wall in the living room, redesigned all the flooring, and changed the wood throughout. "Since we were on a budget, Tino chose this cheap-as-chips pale pine for the doors and walls, and it makes the rooms look fantastic," says the client. "The living room's gray-and-white color scheme with a touch of green is also genius." Meanwhile, Tino's decision to open up the tiny, somber entrance hall onto a newly created dining room made the chalet feel spacious and airy. The kitchen was given priority with access to a terrace because the family spends considerable time there throughout the year. Its new location now allows for al fresco dining on the terrace. "We go a lot in the summer," the client says, "That view—you just can't be bad-tempered sitting there."

BELOW, LEFT
The kitchen was relocated to open onto the terrace with breathtaking views to the Alps beyond, suiting the client's summer excursions. "We designed simple and bleached pine cabinetry, with no hardware to keep with the minimal feel," says Tino. The curtains and blinds are made in a Holland & Sherry linen with blue borders.

BELOW, RIGHT
The blue-glazed lava countertops and backsplash create an other worldly vista onto the cosmos.

FACING PAGE
In the dining room, Tino designed the dining table that can be folded to form a console when not being used, and sourced the 1950s chairs. "The owner's Brazilian feather headdress fits into a specially designed niche and enhances the presence of nature in the natural Alpine paradise," he says.

"TINO IS A FAMILY FRIEND, THERE'S A PERSONAL HISTORY THERE," SAYS THE CLIENT

"TINO LITERALLY REIMAGINED THE WHOLE VIBE OF THE HOUSE. HE GOT TO REALLY ENGAGE IN THE PROJECT," SAYS THE CLIENT

FACING PAGE
Tino redesigned the balustrade for the staircase. "The chalet was very dated, we had to remove the 1970s atmosphere," he says. "All the varnished wood had turned orange. The intent was to give the spaces a more natural feel." The blue wool and jute stair runner is from Holland & Sherry.

ABOVE, LEFT
In the downstairs bathroom, Tino created a gracefully refined sink from a single piece of natural Georgette stone.

ABOVE, RIGHT
A view of the top floor's landing with a Tino Zervudachi-designed plaster "Bucket" hanging light.

RIGHT
A view into the living room from the entrance hall. "Tino was unbelievably practical, no space went to waste," says the client.

FAR LEFT
In the living room,
masculine elegance
features throughout
as exemplified by
a wooden sofa made
in Bali, with luxurious
cashmere cushions.

LEFT
Brown felt curtains
in the gaming area
are edged with cream
bindings and add
a stylish, warm feel.
A contemporary cut-out
metal cuckoo clock
adds charm.

FACING PAGE
The dining area rests
in the corner of the living
room. Tino sourced much
of the furniture when
traveling in Indonesia—
"I was inspired by the
marvelous quality of
the wood," he says—and
was able to link the
Alpine Swiss aesthetic
with traditional Asian
wood-fabrication
techniques, as can
be seen from
this dining table.

ALPINE HUMOR

Nestled in the Alps, this apartment was originally intended as guest accommodation for a client who lived across the way, and who had already commissioned from Tino fifteen other projects all over the world. "Tino is incredibly easygoing and I trust his judgement," he says. Like many winter vacation apartments, it was in a development bought off-plan. Two apartments were combined into one and reimagined to create a highly elegant Alpine bolt-hole, complete with an authentic Finnish sauna heated by a traditional wood-burning stove known as a *kiaus,* and a post-sauna relaxation space. Tino Zervudachi reworked the developer's plans, removing many partitions to create a lofty-ceilinged salon with a seres of small dedicated areas to dine or play backgammon and cards. Creating volume and serenity were equally important, and both were achieved by bringing in light. Tino worked with local carpenters to ensure the right tone of local timber and installed a fireplace with soaring proportions. Different types of seating—such as the Zervudachi-designed Balinese wooden-frame sofas piled with cashmere cushions—were created to give comfort and character. "Tino's chalet work is amazing. His feeling for color and textiles is very warm and masculine," offers the well-travelled client, whose extensive library contributes to the comfortable and cozy feel. The collection of objects reflects his playful sense of humor, as demonstrated by the contemporary Swiss cuckoo clock, papier-mâché hunting trophies, a painting by Christopher Winter, and the carpet design that simulates floorboards. Meanwhile, the narrow, whitewashed corridors highlight the owner's collection of Alpine ski posters. When the work was finished, the client decided the spectacular space was too tempting to resist, and this guest apartment became his own.

RIGHT
Tino created the comfort
of this alpine paradise
by imagining one large
loft-like space. This meant
removing the central
partition that was planned
by the developers, then
designing and installing
the fireplace and
bookcases. Furniture
details include using
steamed wood and
creating glass-top coffee
table made from ancient
railway sleepers.

BELOW
The client's playfulness is captured by his art collection, exemplified by Christopher Winter's graphic painting of two children, a papier-mâché hunting trophy, and a fake cuckoo clock in the gaming area.
An amusing faux floorboard carpet runs throughout the apartment, mixing comfort with a sense of humor.

FACING PAGE
In the hallway, vintage Alpine posters surround another papier-mâché hunting trophy.

"LIKE A MAGICIAN, TINO USED LIGHT, VOLUME, SPACE, COLORS, FURNITURE, AND ART IN ORDER TO ACHIEVE INTERIORS THAT WERE HIGHLY SOPHISTICATED BUT AT THE SAME TIME COOL, FRESH, UNEXPECTED, AND, OF COURSE, ALWAYS COMFORTABLE." CONSTANTIN CANTACUZÈNE

LEFT
The client's requisite—an
authentic, wood-burning
Finnish sauna—was
complicated to achieve.
"Usually this type
of sauna is a cabin in
the snow or on the
ground floor," says Tino.
"It was a challenge
to incorporate it into a
top-floor apartment."

In the après-sauna room, two traditional, boiled-wool sauna hats hang on the wall, beside Jules Wabbes sconces, and generous cushions for post-sauna lounging.

SWISS REFUGE, GSTAAD

Tino Zervudachi has spent many winters going to Gstaad, so when the opportunity arose to acquire a well-located apartment in a newly built chalet, he snapped up the top floor. Five minutes from the town center, the apartment has soaring ceilings and sensational views across protected farmland. Most importantly, this Swiss home has the advantage of facing east and southwest, filling the apartment with sunshine from morning till sundown. Tino was able to design his ideal interior layout, electing to turn the three-bedroom apartment into a comfortable one-bedroom apartment with a study. Seeking a loft-in-a-barn feel, he removed the unnecessary bedrooms and bathrooms, creating an airy living space that is open to the rafters, adding skylights for still more light. The decoration defines Tino's style by being poetically eclectic, mixing tribal artefacts, oriental and African textiles, and unusual objects brought back from his travels. To emphasize the laid-back atmosphere, Tino designed large daybeds instead of sofas. They prove perfect for lounging after a long day's skiing. To his constant delight, from his bathroom, through French doors that look up the valley, Tino can spot the occasional deer running across the mountainside.

TOP, LEFT
Tino's covered balcony is used throughout the year. The view looks onto protected farmland that surrounds the house and the glacier, as well as passing trains. "This protected corner creates a particular atmosphere and makes for perfect viewing towards the open mountains beyond."

BOTTOM, LEFT
Despite looking isolated in the middle of the countryside, this haven is only a few minutes' walk from the center of the village, giving a sense of freedom from and yet connection to it.

FACING PAGE
Tino instills appealing charm in the kitchen and dining area by combining a François-Xavier Lalanne sheep with a Pablo Reinoso chair/tree sculpture. The horizontally laid pine planks were brushed to create textural depth. The intent was to make the kitchen cabinets disappear within the chalet's wall-cladding.

FACING PAGE
Tino's loft-like
atmosphere is enhanced
with built-in daybed,
an ebonized wood
coffee table made of five
different elements to be
pulled out as needed,
and a nineteenth-
century French chaise
recovered with a textile
from Indonesia.
A nineteenth-century
gong, found in Bali,
dominates the
monumental fireplace
that he designed.
On either side, there are
floating shelves for books
and objects, while the
added skylight brightens
up the room.

ABOVE, LEFT
In the living room,
favorite objects include
Setsuko Klossowska
de Rola's *Smoking Cat*
incense burner, an
eighteenth-century
famille verte
porcelain plate, and
a contemporary
crystal light sculpture.

ABOVE, RIGHT
A 1940s duck-shaped
pewter teapot.

LEFT
A corner in the living room continues with inspired Alpine elements such as the Arctander armchair covered with pony skin and a painting by Louise Bourgeois.

FACING PAGE
Under the living room's beams, a series of playful stools are a modernistic take on the traditional milking kind. Watercolor by Marlène Dumas.

FACING PAGE
In the master bathroom with black slate floors, the pine-clad bathtub faces the French doors to the balcony that looks toward the spectacular mountain view.

RIGHT
In a guest bedroom, an eclectic coziness is achieved with a Manuela Zervudachi snowflake wall sculpture, Jean-Michel Frank's narrow console desk, André Sornay's cane chair, and Alexis de la Falaise's glass-top circular table. The silver-fox bed throw adds a sense of luxury while the Tibetan carpet was found on Tino's travels.

AFTERWORD

In going through the process of exposing oneself through a book with a photographic record and an accompanying text showing and describing the work that I have been fortunate enough to be asked to do for so many clients over many years (and for some clients, over and over again), I cannot help but feel that interior design is more than anything a conversation. It is a committed collaboration between the client and design team and artisans, to achieve the house owner's dream home, by listening very carefully to their wishes and channeling their visons towards design solutions that will make them happy, and really help them create their individual environment.

The interior designer's role is to bring those dreams to life through experience and design knowledge with the help of the rest of the design team—the architects, the landscape designers and other consultants—carefully orchestrating, like a conductor or a film director does, all the different artists, artisans and trades to make a harmonious whole that suits the client's character. The result of any project should, in my opinion, be more the expression of the client's unique vision of how they want to live than a portrait of the designer.

As such, I see every project as being unique, even if it is for the same client, because different homes are inherently always different from each other and certainly clients are all different from each other, with different expectations, aspirations, lifestyles and approaches to their homes. This is what makes the work interesting for me and my teams to do; every project is a learning process, and adds a layer of knowledge to our experience that helps contribute to the next project.

Some of the work in this book will hopefully appeal to some of its viewers and readers and might help them to see how the same design approach—the great care needed over interior architecture that houses the decoration and furnishings, and the great care taken over the client's wishes—can lead to such different interiors.

So, I would like to dedicate this book to all the clients who have been so kind as to initially ask me to help make interiors for them, giving me the opportunity each and every time to learn so much from them about how different people like to live, and also for them accepting that their homes be in this book.

ACKNOWLEDGMENTS

I would like to thank all the people who have been involved in all these projects.
The architects: Libe Camarena, Chaletbau Matti, Pietro Cicognani, Sébastien Desroches, Ferguson & Shamamian, Agatha Habjan, Peter Helletzgruber, J.O. Alts, Bruno Jori, Aude Kaemmerlen, Kengo Kuma, Marugg & Hanselmann AG, Nate McBride, Christopher Miners, Laurent Minot, Chris Mitchell, Andrew Oyen, Dimitris Papacharalampous and contractor Petros Kritikos, Purcell, Max Rieder, Kiko Sanchez, Annabelle Selldorf, Oscar Shamamian, Adam Smuszkowicz, Torres Torres, and Samiir Wheaton.
The landscape architects: Louis Benech, Miranda Brooks, Reed Hildebrand, Juan Macedo, Libby Russell, Seppia, and all the other design consultants.
I also express my gratitude to all the artists, artisans and manufacturers of every nature, all of whom have put their knowledge, experience and heart into creating the many varied parts of these interiors, so complex to achieve: Shyam Ahuja, Philippe Anthonioz, Bartholomeus, Antoine Broccardo, Howard Chairs, Laurent Chwast, Colnaghi, Christophe Delcourt, André Dubreuil, François-Xavier Dutruc-Rosset, Frozen Music, Florence Girette, Galerie Diurne, Gerratts, Francois Goffinet, Sylvie Johnson, Kathy Jones, Jean-François Lesage, Valentine Loellmann, Lilou Marquand, Maximiliano Modesti, Nelly Munthe, Christian Mussy, Passementerie Declercq, Phelippeau Tapissier, Éric Philippe, Pouenat, Claude Schaer, Schmidt & Cie, Alain Simonnot, Benjamin Steinitz, T.C.K.W, Techniques Transparentes, Manuela Zervudachi, and to all the collaborators in my different offices: in Paris, Antoine de Sigy, Ohm Wittawat Chulsukon, and Marie-Astrid Piron; in London, Jason Roberts, Laurence Macadam, and Hugh Henry; in New York, Lucy Singh. And, of course, Constantin Cantacuzene. Finally, I thank Flammarion, Suzanne Tise-Isoré, Bernard Lagacé, and Lara Lo Calzo, as well Natasha A. Fraser and Polly Stuart-Mills for their patience with me in getting this book done, and all the photographers who have contributed to making this book happen, with special thanks to Derry Moore for his foreword and for leading me to becoming an interior designer in the first place.

The publisher and the Style & Design team express their sincere gratitude to Tino Zervudachi for allowing them to accompany him on this wonderful project, and to Natasha A. Fraser for her passion and expertise. The publisher would also like to acknowledge Antoine de Sigy for his support and Polly Stuart-Mills for her invaluable and steadfast work throughout.